SPIRITUAL REFLECTIONS

on Faith, Values, and Culture

Peace & Blessings,

[signature]

CLAY STAUFFER

First edition: January 2019

ISBN 978-0-578-41684-7

To my Family:
Megan, Montgomery, Clayton, and Wade.
You mean the world to me!

&

To the members of Woodmont Christian Church in
Nashville, TN on the church's 75th anniversary.
You once took a chance on a young Senior Minister
who was only 27 at the time. I will always be grateful.

Contents

SPIRITUAL REFLECTIONS

INTRODUCTION

On Friday afternoon, September 2nd, 2005, I was boarding a plane in Memphis, TN to fly west to Norman, OK to meet some old college friends and watch my alma mater TCU play the Oklahoma Sooners in football the following day. I was standing in line, about to give the attendant my ticket when my cell phone rang. It was my sister. She was crying hysterically. She had found a suicide note on the dining room table from our mother but could not find our mom. I immediately left the airport. I knew we would either be checking my mother back into a hospital for a third time or planning her funeral. By the time I made it back to my childhood home, there were police cars, an ambulance, and a fire truck in the driveway. I knew exactly what had happened. My mother was dead.

I was only twenty-five years old at the time, had just graduated from Princeton Seminary, was ordained into the ministry, and had moved back to my hometown. Now I was living a nightmare. My parents were divorced, and I was the oldest of four children. My mother had battled depression for years. It had only grown worse over time. She had basically given up on life. Mental illness is real and devastating. As her children, we were now left to pick up the pieces. Over a thousand people came to her visitation a few days later. We had her funeral the following day at our home church. It was all surreal, like a bad dream but you don't wake up. We laid her to rest in her hometown of Paris, TN, right next to her father. My life had changed.

Going through something like this makes you wrestle with the bigger questions of life. Why are we here? Why is there so much pain and hurt? Where is God when we need him? How do we find meaning and purpose? Socrates once said, "The unexamined life is not worth living." I believe that. But answering these questions and holding on to faith is not always easy. I made the difficult decision to stick with the ministry but all of these questions remained on my mind. These questions don't have easy answers. I wanted to use my pain to help others deal with their own.

Two years later, I was called to serve as the Senior Minister of Woodmont Christian Church in Nashville, TN at the age of twenty-seven. Woodmont is a congregation with a rich history, a mix of denominational backgrounds, politics, and ideologies. It is full of community leaders, movers, shakers, and intelligent individuals. Over the past decade, I have also written a regular column that appears on Saturdays in the "Faith and Values" section of The Tennessean. I attempt to be a balanced voice in what is viewed by many as a progressive newspaper. My writing tends to focus on issues of faith, values, spirituality, meaning, and American culture. I have a keen interest in each of these areas and find that there is clear overlap. Perhaps every generation says this, but we continue to live in very interesting times. Our age has been referred to as "secular" or even "post-Christian" by many scholars. Some churches thrive while other churches struggle. Faith is still very important but varies from Christian to Christian. There is no clear consensus on what it means to be "Christian." Many, especially in the millennial generation, consider themselves "spiritual but not religious," but what does this really imply? What does it mean to grow spiritually? What does it mean to do meaningful soul work? What are the values and priorities that should matter most? What type of culture will our children and grandchildren inherit? Here are a few insights that I believe to be true.

- *Life is about the journey and not the destination.*
- *All human beings long for meaning and deeper purpose in their lives.*
- *Jesus Christ continues to speak to and challenge our culture.*
- *Issues of character and integrity are very important.*
- *Growth in the spiritual life has become much more challenging in this busy age of technology, multi-tasking, and over-commitment.*
- *Relationships are essential and can cause great joy and fulfillment as well as pain and heartache.*
- *Politics and ideology have become both polarizing and toxic in many ways, deeply dividing families and friendships.*
- *Wisdom is much more valuable than knowledge.*
- *Social isolation and loneliness will continue to be one of the great challenges of the twenty-first century.*
- *We live in an age of anxiety, where fear abounds and overwhelms many.*
- *We all long to move beyond superficiality to a much deeper level of connection.*
- *Social media is not an adequate substitute for authentic relationships and community*
- *Being present in the moment has become a major challenge in the digital age.*
- *Certain values must be passed down from generation to generation.*

This book is a collection of articles and essays from years of writing, speaking, and research. Many of these reflections have been published as columns in *The Tennessean* over the years, and others represent new insights and reflections. While many books will focus on one particular subject area or topic, this book intentionally covers a lot of ground. It is divided into six basic sections. First, "Wisdom" that can be applied to daily living and the challenges that we all face. Second, "Values" that are both timeless and important for every generation. The third section contains reflections on "The Christian Life," what it is, and what it means. The fourth section focuses on "Spirituality" and the inner work of the soul that we are called to do. The fifth section deals with politics and American Culture and how politics is both important and polarizing at the same time. Lastly, the sixth section contains spiritual reflections on many newsworthy events that have happened around the world in recent years. It is my prayer that these writings will be used for both personal growth and group conversation inside and outside of the church.

—*Clay Stauffer*
Nashville, TN
Christmas 2018

I

WISDOM FOR LIFE

1. The Inevitability of Change

Years ago, the Byrds sang, "To everything, turn, turn, turn." It has truly been bizarre to be a pastor in the days following the 2016 presidential election. I have been with people who are excited, and I have been with people who are heartbroken. I have talked to people who believe our country was saved, and I have talked to people who believe our country is falling apart. I have seen joy, and I have seen fear. I have seen jubilation, and I have seen devastation. It reminds me of the way Charles Dickens begins his famous novel: "It was the best of times, it was the worst of times." This has been called a change election, and one thing we know for sure is that life is full of change. The question has never been, "Will things change in life?" The question has always been, "How will we deal with change?" Governments change, marriages change, friendships change, children change, finances change, health changes, and we all change. Not a single one of us is the same person we were a year ago, five years ago, or ten years ago. With change comes loss and grief, and that is the hardest part.

For years, I have given Jerry Sittser's book *A Grace Disguised* to those who have lost loved ones and are grieving. Sittser says, "Living means changing, and change requires we lose one thing before we gain something else. We lose our youth but gain adulthood. We lose the security of home but gain the independence of being on our own. We lose the freedom of singleness but gain the intimacy of marriage. We lose a daughter but gain a son-in-law. Life is a constant succession of losses and gains." Of course, not all change is good, and humans are notorious for reminiscing about the "good old days." But sometimes the good old days are figments of our imagination.

In those times we struggled, we feared, and we worried, but often we forget that part of it. I moved to Nashville over nine years ago as a young, single pastor with a golden retriever and a moving trailer holding my earthly possessions. Now I am married with three children. Life is very different. One of the reasons we don't like change is because we prefer to be in control. We prefer the predictable to the unpredictable, the certain to the uncertain, the known to the unknown. Richard Rohr says, "As we grow older, we become control freaks. A need to be in charge moves us deeper and deeper into a world of anxiety." There is no question that fear and anxiety has become the defining challenge of our age. It is a spiritual hurdle. But along with change comes the opportunity for growth. Every new stage of life brings new possibilities for renewal and rebirth. It comes down to our mindset. How will we approach the future? Sittser says, "The soul is elastic, like a balloon. It can grow larger through suffering. Loss can enlarge its capacity for anger, depression, despair, and anguish, all natural and legitimate emotions whenever we experience loss. Once enlarged, the soul is also capable of experiencing greater joy, peace strength, and love." So whenever change comes in any form, for good or bad, we get to decide whether or not we will grow.

2. Wisdom from Generation to Generation

Recently, I sat around the table with about twenty "seasoned" men from our church. Most of them are now retired and in their seventies or eighties, and I was interested in picking their brains about life and what they have learned and experienced throughout the years. I am convinced that many in the younger generations do not take the time to soak up wisdom from those who now have the advantage of reflecting back upon their lives. They have fought the battles, learned the lessons, and have the scars and character to show it. My question to them was simple and straightforward: "What is your best life advice for the next generation, and do you have any regrets?" Here are some of the things that were shared:

Seek God first and develop a spiritual life at a young age. Don't work too hard at the expense of your family. Find the sacred balance between work and family. Enjoy every stage of life as it comes because it goes by all too quickly, and you can't turn back the clock. Be kind to everyone because kindness is a form of love. Treat others the way you want to be treated. Work hard but then play hard. Make faith a priority in your marriage and family life. Be proud but not prideful, confident but not arrogant. Maturity comes with years. Disappointment is inevitable. Be gentle and compassionate. Try to become somebody that you yourself will admire. Be optimistic and positive. Don't dwell too much on the past which you cannot change. Learn to enjoy what you're doing so you never have to work a day in your life. Guard your reputation and don't compromise your character. Stay focused on meaningful objectives and live with the end in mind. Beware of seeking instant gratification. Many of the things worth doing take a long and sustained effort. Lead by example. Don't ask others to do things you wouldn't do. Be humble and keep your ego in check. Learn to live within your means. Money is not the answer to everything. Remember that relationships matter most, so learn to nurture them and invest in them. Take nothing for granted, and beware of developing an entitlement mindset. Spend quality time with your children because they will grow up fast. Carve out regular time to nurture the soul. Travel with your family whenever possible to make memories that will last forever. Give it your all, whether at work or at home. Follow the example of Christ. Take care of your health at a young age because it only gets more challenging. Marry somebody who can put you in your place whenever necessary. Cultivate friendships that will last a life time. Tell the truth, even when it's hard and inconvenient. Be true to yourself and be the same person no matter who you might be around. Love others even when they've hurt you, and don't forget the importance of forgiveness and letting things go. Approach every day as a gift because we never know about tomorrow. Don't worry constantly and needlessly. Trust that things will turn out okay, even if it's not what you had planned.

I'm deeply grateful to these men for their wisdom and insight. My hope and prayer is that younger generations will continue to learn and gain wisdom from those who have gone before us.

3. Balancing the Ego and the Soul

It's hard to argue that we live in a materialistic world. It's been said before that "we buy things we don't need with money we don't have to impress people we don't really care about." Growing secularization has only enhanced our obsession with money and toys. Even honestly pursuing the American Dream (however that is defined) throws us into an endless cycle of competition, consumption, comparison, and stress. Social media, despite its benefits, keeps us ever aware of what others have that we don't. Stanley Hauerwas and Will Willimon say, "Desire is both contagious and imitative. I want this or that because someone else wants this or that. That we learn desire from one another means that we desperately desire one another's approval, even though our desires put us in envious conflict with one another. We think of life as a zero-sum game. Accordingly, we want what our neighbor has, and we are led to an endless cycle of acquisition that never satisfies." There is absolutely nothing wrong with working hard, achieving success, being compensated fairly, providing for your family, and building a better life. But remember, it's the same desire to accomplish and achieve that keeps us restless and unsatisfied in our spiritual lives. We tend to neglect our soul.

In his book *Everything Belongs*, Richard Rohr talks about the ongoing struggle between the ego and the soul. He says, "The primary philosophical and spiritual problem in the West is the lie of individualism. Individualism makes church almost impossible. It makes community almost impossible. It makes compassion almost impossible. Life is not about me; it is about God, and God is about love. When we don't know love, when we don't experience love, when we experience only the insecurity and fragility of the small self, we become restless." Restlessness is an ongoing spiritual problem for many today. People are restless with themselves. They are restless in their marriages. They are restless with their jobs. We address that restlessness in a variety of ways—excessive eating, drinking, medicating, shopping, smoking, working, and worrying. These are symptoms of a much deeper problem that lies within.

Jesus teaches us in the Sermon on the Mount that it's our inner attitudes and intentions that matter; What is going on in the head and heart. When we neglect the soul, problems abound. Rohr says that many people today "live in a disenchanted universe without meaning, purpose, or direction." That is sad. How can that be changed? Perhaps it starts with understanding that what satisfies the ego does not satisfy the soul. What keeps us relevant in the marketplace is not really what gives us meaning. Life must be about more than work. Life must be more than success. Life must be more than getting rich. Life must be more than climbing the social ladder. Life must be more than always being right. Maybe he who dies with the most toys actually loses, especially if he is enjoying them alone. Human beings have done one heck of a job coming up with things to keep us busy, distracted, and feeling important, and perhaps that's the problem. In our relentless attempt to feed the ego, the soul is neglected.

4. Our Quest for Meaning

Rabbi Jonathan Sacks published a book last year titled *Not In God's Name: Confronting Religious Violence*. It's certainly a relevant book given the dangerous world in which we now live. He says this: "Science, technology, the free market, and the liberal democratic state have enabled us to reach unprecedented achievements in knowledge, freedom, life expectancy, and affluence. They are among the greatest achievements of human civilization and are to be defended and cherished. But they do not and cannot answer three questions every reflective individual will ask at some time in his or her life: Who am I? Why I am I here? How then shall I live?" Religion matters because it is hard to live without meaning. Faith and spirituality are dependent upon wrestling with these questions.

A few years ago, an article appeared in *The Atlantic* by Emily Smith. The title of the article was "There's More to Life Than Being Happy." She refers to Holocaust survivor Victor Frankl's 1946 book, *Man's Search for Meaning*, and she talks about the basic difference between "meaning" and "happiness." She says, "Happiness without meaning characterizes a relatively shallow, self-absorbed, or even selfish life in which things go well, needs and desires are easily satisfied, and difficult or taxing estranglements are avoided." Having an abundance of money and possessions may bring about temporary happiness, but in and of itself, it will not provide meaning in life. She continues, "Happiness comes and goes but meaning has longevity. People whose lives have high levels of meaning often actively seek meaning out even when they know it will come at the expense of happiness." In other words, some of the things that give us meaning in life—sacrifice, friendship, marriage, raising children, sustaining a career—may even bring about unhappiness at times because these things require commitment and hard work. Meaning is much deeper, and it has staying power. The article argues that happiness is basically associated with taking, but meaning is associated with giving. Happiness is fleeting, meaning is ongoing. Happiness often results from things out of our control, meaning is something that we choose. Every single one of us likes to be happy, but we all long for meaning. And yes, it is possible to experience both. Victor Frankl once said, "Being human always points, and is directed to something or someone other than oneself. The more one forgets himself by giving himself a cause to serve or another person to love—the more human he is."

David Brooks posed similar questions in his book *The Road to Character*. These are questions that we should all ask over and over again: "Toward what should I orient my life? Who am I, and what is my nature? How do I mold my nature to make it gradually better day by day? What virtues are the most important to cultivate, and what weaknesses should I fear the most? How can I raise my children with a true sense of who they are and a practical set of ideas about how to travel along the road to character?" What we seem to have in our world today is a deep longing for meaning and many answers that seem insufficient. What we need is a reorientation to what life is all about. If we can move beyond the noise and many distractions, we can begin to answer these timeless yet profound questions in our own day.

5. *How Well Do You Know Yourself?*

It's been said before that we are mysteries unto ourselves. The Apostle Paul writes those famous words to the Romans: "I do not understand my own actions, for I do not do what I want, but I do the very thing that I hate." In other words, we often know what we should do, but we fail to do it. Why? Could it be that we need to gain a better understanding of ourselves? Who we are? What motivates us? What challenges us? What scares us? How do we behave in times of stress and strength? How do we see the world? How do others see us? These are all important questions as we seek to live spiritually and form meaningful relationships with other people. The quality of our relationships will determine the quality of our lives. The Enneagram is an ancient personality typing system. It is over 2000 years old, but it was not written down until the 1970's. It helps us come to terms with our own personalities and "why we do what we do." Our personality is the way we cope in the world and it often hides our true essence - who God created us to be. According to Ian Morgan Cron and Susan Stabile, we all have one number, and it was basically determined by the time we were five years old. However, we will certainly resonate with one or two other numbers and may have a hard time determining exactly what our numbers are. Here are the nine different personality types:

TYPE 1—The Perfectionist: Ethical, dedicated and reliable, they are motivated by a desire to live the right way, improve the world, and avoid fault and blame. Their deadly sin is ANGER that really manifests itself in RESENTMENT.

TYPE 2—The Helper: Warm, caring, and giving, they are

motivated by a need to be loved and needed, and to avoid acknowledging their own needs. The deadly sin of TWO's is PRIDE, and TWO's often relish in the myth of their own indispensability.

TYPE 3—The Performer: Success oriented, image conscious and wired for productivity, they are motivated by a need to be (or appear to be) successful and to avoid failure. The deadly sin of THREE's is DECEIT—not that they deceive others but they often deceive themselves into thinking that they are what they accomplish.

TYPE 4—The Romantic: Creative, sensitive and moody, they are motivated by a need to be understood, experience their oversized feelings, and avoid being ordinary. The deadly sin of FOUR's is ENVY. They can envy the normalcy, happiness, and sense of comfort with which others live their lives.

TYPE 5—The Investigator: Analytical, detached, and private, they are motivated by a need to gain knowledge, conserve energy and avoid relying on others. The deadly sin of FIVE's is AVARICE, or a desire to clench and protect what little they already have.

TYPE 6—The Loyalist: Committed, practical, and witty, they are worst case scenario thinkers who are motivated by fear and the need for security. The Deadly sin of SIX's is FEAR, and fear and anxiety can often take over their lives.

TYPE 7—The Enthusiast: Fun, spontaneous, and adventurous, they are motivated by a need to be happy, to plan stimulating experiences and to avoid pain. Their deadly sin is GLUTTONY, especially as they devour and consume positive experiences.

TYPE 8—The Challenger: Commanding, intense, and confrontational, they are motivated by a need to be strong and avoid feeling weak or vulnerable. The deadly sin of EIGHT's is LUST, not lust in a sexual sense but lust for control.

TYPE 9—The Peacemaker: Pleasant, laid back, and accommodating, they are motivated by a need to keep the peace, merge with others, and avoid conflict. The deadly sin of NINE's is SLOTH, which is really related to their lack of passion and motivation. (Cron & Stabile, *The Road Back To You* pp. 25-26)

No one personality type is better than any other, just different. We live in a world where, perhaps more than ever before, people need to work towards understanding each other better in marriages, families, neighborhoods, churches, politics, and in business. We are often quick to judge and slow to listen. There is a lot of anger, fear, and hostility in our culture. The Enneagram has the potential to open our eyes so that we can live more peacefully and better "love our neighbors as ourselves."

6. Wisdom for Graduates

May is a month of graduations. "Commencement" actually means beginning. It's the beginning of the next chapter of life. Here are some thoughts for those moving on to life's next stage, whatever it might be. Change is inevitable, but growth is optional. Everything in life changes, but we get to decide whether or not we will grow in the process. Those who are wise embrace change as an adventure, a challenge, and an opportunity. Relationships are the key to happiness. The quality of your relationships determines the quality of your life. People don't care how much you know until they first know that you care. Trust is the currency of relationships. Love your family, even when it's hard. Build friendships on a regular basis. Pay attention to the people in your inner circle because they will influence you for better or worse. Learn to forgive. Forgiveness is not just a Christian virtue but a recipe for sanity and survival in life. If you don't forgive and let go, your past will control you and wear you down. Forgiveness is a gift to others and to yourself. Everybody experiences pain because it's part of the human condition. But the way we process and handle our pain makes all the difference. Pain that goes unaddressed will manifest itself in unhealthy ways. Anger is real but dangerous. Words can hurt. Pay attention to what comes out of your mouth. Think before you speak. Attitude matters. There is incredible power in positive thinking, and we all get to choose what our focus will be. Criticism and negativity are tempting and easy. Offer solutions. Live in hope and spread hope to others. Be a peacemaker. Remember that you cannot spread peace until you first have it in your own heart. Prayer and meditation are essential. Extremes are dangerous. The world needs more moderates who can get along with others. Civility has been on a rapid decline in our culture. Respect others' opinions but maintain your convictions. Keep faith alive. Faith does not mean that God will line everything up the way you plan, but it does mean that everything will work out. Faith allows us to deal with the reality that we are not in control of many things. Live life one day at a time—not in the past, not in the future. The present is all we have, so don't take it for granted. Cultivate the fruits of the spirit—love, joy, peace, patience, kindness, generosity, faithfulness, gentleness, and self-control. This is the litmus test for progress in the spiritual life. Live the Golden Rule. Speak up for those without a voice—the poor, the marginalized, the powerless. Do justice, love kindness, and maintain humility. Find your own definition of success. Remember that money is not everything. It makes a great servant but a terrible master. Match your passion with the needs of the world. Be slow to judge others because you never know what they might be going through. Make love a verb and not just a noun. Don't fall apart when you are criticized. Keep your ego in check. Draw the line between confidence and arrogance. Don't forget to tend to your soul. Enjoy the journey that is life because we never know how long it will last.

7. Spiritual Insights for Graduates

Graduation is a time to reflect and look head. Graduates are seeking wisdom and guidance as they move ahead to life's next chapter and venture into the unknown future. Living by the Golden Rule can serve any person well, but here are some addition reflections for the journey ahead.

- Life is a gift and not a burden. Even on bad days, we have so much to be thankful for.
- Love is a choice and an action. It involves risk, perseverance, sacrifice, and hard work. Love drives out fear.
- God is working in ways that we cannot even begin to understand.
- Pain and suffering are real, but they always make us stronger.
- Admitting we are wrong from time to time is necessary and healthy.
- Technology is both a blessing and a danger. It will run and even ruin our lives if we let it. Social media is a great way to connect but can quickly lead to narcissism.
- Be realistic about taking on commitments. Being busy has become a sign of status. Sometimes simplifying our lives is the best option.
- Money can buy lots of things but it cannot buy happiness and meaning. Many wealthy people are miserable and have not figured out the meaning of life. We all create idols in life without even knowing it.
- Knowledge is power, but it's different from wisdom. Personal growth is essential.
- Theology is a life-long endeavor. God cannot be put into a box.

- We should never say things about other people that we wouldn't want them to hear. If we say it, we should be willing to stand by it.
- Materialism and a false sense of self-sufficiency is an ongoing temptation in North America. The more affluent the society, the more distractions to real faith. Christ was right: "Where your treasure is, there your heart will be also." Heart follows treasure. Money makes a great servant but a terrible master.
- The government is not the answer to every problem, but it is responsible for certain things. Hateful partisanship and incivility have the potential to tear our nation apart from the inside out. Neither Republicans nor Democrats have a monopoly on truth. Labels are dangerous. Civility is admirable.
- The birth lottery is real. Some are born to privilege. Some are born to poverty. If you're born on third base, don't act like you hit a triple. Be humble and grateful every day.
- Fear and anxiety must be faced, acknowledged, and sometimes medicated. Anxiety is simply fear of the unknown and will ruin the present.
- Tell the truth because lying is a slippery slope. Truth seems to be in short supply.
- Don't judge people based on their age, religion, or skin color. We can always gain insight from those who are different.
- The United States is a wonderful country, but it's not the only nation under God.
- Travel to new places. Expand your worldview. Don't stay in a bubble.

- Perception is not always reality. Accusations can be false. Rumors can ruin somebody's reputation. Group think is dangerous. Always check the source.
- Credibility is built over time. Trust is built over a life time.
- Love your family, even when it's hard. Forgiveness is a recipe for survival.
- Be thankful for friends, for they are one of life's greatest treasures.
- Pray regularly. Eat healthy. Exercise often. Read to learn. Hope. Dream. Listen intently. Be slow to speak and slow to anger. Live life one day at a time. Plan for the future but don't obsess about it.
- The grass may seem greener elsewhere, but usually, it's not.
- Learn from the past, dream for the future, and live in the present.

8. Political, Spiritual, and Moral Wisdom

Mahatma Gandhi was the preeminent leader of Indian independence. His method of choice? Non-violent, civil disobedience. He was deeply concerned with matters of peace and justice and remained committed to these values until his assassination on January 30, 1948. Gandhi once famously said, "I would have been a Christian if not for all the Christians." He named the "Seven Blunders of the World that Lead to Violence" and gave them to his grandson days before his assassination. These are now etched into human history, still speaking to our modern world. **1) Wealth without Work** This could be defined as "getting something for nothing." Think of Wall Street scandals, ponzi schemes, and shady business deals. Also, think of able bodies who simply choose to work the system. Ours is a "get rich fast" culture and many are not willing to work hard in the process, doing the bare minimum to get by and wanting to reap the rewards without paying the price. **2) Pleasure without Conscience** It's a culture obsessed with sex and sexuality. More and more children are born out of wedlock which often leads to other problems. Many believe, "if it feels good, do it!" Worry about the consequences later. Educational problems often originate with the breakdown of the family and the lack of responsible parenting. Teachers can only do so much with little support in the home. **3) Knowledge without Character** There is an abundance of knowledge, but is there any wisdom? Bernard of Clairvaux once said: "There are those who seek knowledge for the sake of knowledge; that is curiosity. There are those who seek knowledge to be known by others; that is vanity. There are those who seek knowledge in order to serve; that is love." Are we growing and loving while we are learning? **4) Commerce without Morality** How are employees treated? Are they paid a fair wage and shown respect? It is possible to succeed in business, remain ethical, and treat people fairly. Many do it well. Jesus said, "What good is it to gain the whole world but forfeit your life?" There is more to life than chasing the almighty dollar. **5) Science without Humanity** The technological advances in the medical world are astounding. It becomes tempting for humans to think that they can play God. Science should strengthen faith. **6) Worship without Sacrifice** As our culture becomes more individualized, sacrificing to help others may seem like a foreign concept. Many choose to worship the mirror. Phillips Brooks says, "Over the past several decades we have built a moral ecology around the Big Me, around the belief in a golden figure inside. This has led to a rise in narcissism and self-aggrandizement." Jesus taught, "Deny self." How popular is that? **7) Politics without Principle** What are we willing to stand for and speak up for? What issues really matter? Do moderates still have a place at the table or have they been drowned out by all the crazies? When do we quit fighting so that we can compromise and work together? Governing and leadership have always required compromise. Gandhi once prayed: "I offer you peace. I offer you love. I offer you friendship. I see your beauty. I hear your need. I feel your feelings. My wisdom flows from the Highest Source. I salute that Source in you. Let us work together for unity and love."

9. Living Life with Few Regrets

The year 2013 is almost history. What will you remember about the past twelve months? North Korea's ongoing nuclear threat? The rise of Pope Francis? The death of Margaret Thatcher—the "Iron Lady"? The Boston Marathon Bombings? The antics of Edward Snowden? Deadly tornadoes ripping through Oklahoma? The Vanderbilt rape scandal? Detroit's bankruptcy? The local debate over AMP? Partisan gridlock in Washington? Ted Cruz? George Zimmerman? Miley Cyrus? The US Government shutdown? The surging stock market? The crisis in Syria? The devastating Typhoon in the Philippines? The rise of Duck Dynasty? The controversial words of Phil Robertson and Cracker Barrel's dilemma? Problems with the Affordable Care Act rollout? The death and legacy of Nelson Mandela? What sticks out in your mind?

The close of a year is an ideal time to reflect and look ahead, to learn from the past and hope for the future. What have we learned? How have we changed? What will we do better next year? Socrates is famous for saying that "the unexamined life is not worth living." I agree. We are all responsible for analyzing our own lives and doing whatever we can to improve and change for the better. Many books and articles have been published on the top regrets people have in life. The research is always fascinating, showing that many people regret specific things in their later years: working too much at the expense of family and friendships; not standing up to bullies in school and in life; not staying in touch with some good friends from childhood and youth; not turning off the phone more or simply leaving it at home; breaking up with a true love; worrying about what others think so much; a lack of self-confidence; living the life that my parents wanted me to live instead of the one I wanted to; not applying for that "dream job" I always wanted; not being happier more often; taking life too seriously; not going on more trips with family and friends; letting a marriage break down; not teaching my kids to do more things; not burying the hatchet with a family member or old friend; not trusting that voice in the back of my head more; not asking that girl or boy out; getting involved with the wrong group of friends when I was younger; not getting that degree; choosing the practical job over the one I really wanted; not spending more time with the kids; not taking care of my health when I had the chance; not having the courage to get up and talk at a funeral or important event; not visiting a dying friend before he died; not learning another language; and not being a better father or mother. Do any of these resonate with you?

On the first Sunday of every New Year, I always preach a sermon titled "This I Believe." Based on Jesus' parable of the wise and foolish builder in the Sermon on the Mount (Matthew 7), I will share with the congregation my core convictions and beliefs and challenge them to think about their own. Here's what that list includes for me: I believe in God. I believe in love. I believe in Jesus Christ and the fellowship of the Church (though it is far from perfect). I believe in the Bible as speaking God's truth (I don't worship the Bible. I worship God.). I believe in the mysterious power of prayer. I believe in marriage, home, and family life. I believe in free will. I believe in life after death. The truth is we all build our lives on a certain foundation. And when the storms of life come, and they will, our foundations get tested.

We live in a rapidly changing world where many people are lost and long to find meaning. Anxiety and fear are always present. We seem to base everything on money and status. Materialism and consumerism run rampant. We often love things and use people as opposed to loving people and using things. Ironically, our digital age that is supposed to be connecting us is leaving us lonelier than ever before. Many people are searching for meaning and they tend to confuse it with happiness. It is now more important than ever before to name our beliefs, our priorities, our convictions, and do our very best to live by them. Show me your calendar and your bank statement and I will tell you what is most important in your life. The younger generations can sense hypocrisy and pretentiousness immediately. Faith matters. Family matters. Friendships matter. We are often confused about the real meaning of success and what it really is. Perhaps Emerson said it best: "To laugh often and love much; to win the respect of intelligent persons and the affection of children; to earn the approbation of honest citizens and endure the betrayal of false friends; to appreciate beauty; to find the best in others; to give of one's self; to leave the world a bit better, whether by a healthy child, a garden patch or a redeemed social condition; to have played and laughed with enthusiasm and sung with exultation; to know even one life has breathed easier because you have lived—this is to have succeeded." Life will always be about the journey and not the destination. We should always remember that. With each New Year comes new opportunities. So farewell 2013. It's been fun. Here's to a new beginning!

10. Two Halves of Life

Hardly ever will somebody be on his death bed and wish that he had spent more time at the office putting deals together. However, the reality is many in our culture tend to measure life based simply on career and performance, toys, and net worth. It's as if we lack the creativity to think of another way. People like Richard Rohr and Bob Buford talk about the two halves of life. The first half is spent building, establishing, achieving, and creating the container. The second half is spent trying to figure out the meaning and purpose of it all. The first half seems full of stress, worry, and grinding it out. The second half is more spiritual and reflective. Most people make the shift at different times. Some never do. But what is the end goal? If money and achievement is the only means by which we measure our lives, we will forever be disappointed. There is always more to attain. But if relationships and deeper meaning can become the focus, we can tame our restlessness and desires.

Harvard professor Clayton Christiansen raised the question as the title of a book: *How Will You Measure Your Life?* Early on, Christiansen saw the dangers of only defining success by the world's standards. He encountered CEO's and executives who were very rich but lost, successful but empty. They had no meaningful relationships. Their marriages were in shambles. Their friends were superficial. Their children had written them off. Therefore, he made a decision to incorporate the education of character and ethics into his business classes. He says, "Intimate, loving, and enduring relationships with our family and close friends will be among the sources of the deepest joy in our lives." It's also the secret to finding inner peace. The sooner we can make the shift to the second half of life, the better off we will be. It's not a matter of age but a matter of mindset and priority. Spiritual maturity begins with humility, priorities, and the realization that others don't control you. We choose our focus. Ralph Waldo Emerson's definition of success is worth noting: "To laugh often and much; to win the respect of intelligent people and the affection of children; to earn the appreciation of honest critics and endure the betrayal of false friends; to appreciate beauty, to find the best in others; to leave the world a bit better, whether by a healthy child a garden patch or redeemed social condition; to know even one life has breathed easier because you have lived. This is to have succeeded."

11. Finding Resilience in the Face of Pain

I believe there are certain truths that are universal for almost all of us as human beings. First, we all want to be loved, appreciated, and respected. Second, we all search for meaning and purpose in our lives, and we want our lives to matter and make a difference. Third, we all seek to form and sustain meaningful relationships with other people because we are social creatures by our very nature. Fourth, we all want to experience happiness, in whatever way we understand that concept. Fifth, we all have to deal with pain, disappointment, and heartache no matter who we are. Our pain may come from various sources: illness, divorce, depression, addiction, loneliness, infidelity, loss of a spouse, grief, financial challenges, and a host of other things. Although some experience far more than others, nobody gets a pass when it comes to pain. In the face of pain, we are called to be resilient, to bounce back, not to let the trying times of life define us.

The Apostle Paul writes, "Suffering produces endurance, and endurance produces character, and character produces hope, and hope will not disappoint." However, there are certain times in life when we do feel hopeless, as if everything is lost. There are certain times in life when we feel overwhelmed and can't press forward. These are the times when we need to cultivate a resilient spirit and reach out for help. The American Psychological Association once defined resilience in the following way: "The process of adapting well in the face of adversity, trauma, tragedy, threats or significant sources of stress — such as family and relationship problems, serious health problems or workplace, and financial stressors. It means 'bouncing back' from difficult experiences." Yet we must acknowledge that bouncing back is not easy, especially in situations of tragedy, extreme heartache, and great loss.

In 2002, Diane Coutu wrote an article for *The Harvard Business Review* entitled "How Resilience Works." She said that resilient people have three defining characteristics. First, they accept the harsh realities that are facing them. Second, they are able to find meaning in terrible times. And third, they have an uncanny ability to improvise and make due with whatever is at hand. They are survivors. What many fail to understand is that resilience is a skill that must be developed in life. It is similar to faith, spirituality, and emotional intelligence. There are specific things that all of us can do to become more resilient, including:

- Making strong connections with family and friends so they will be there when we need them
- Not seeing any crisis as an insurmountable problem
- Accepting that change is simply a part of life and we can't fight it all the time
- Recognizing that any hardship brings an opportunity for us to grow and become stronger
- Keeping things in perspective in order to avoid catastrophic thinking
- Maintaining a hopeful and positive attitude during difficult times
- Learning to take care of ourselves; self-care is not selfish

A resilient spirit can be developed over time, and each of these ideas can move us in that direction. What is universal is that we all experience pain and heartache. The difference lies with how we respond to it and whether or not we let it define us.

12. Choosing to Grow Through Pain

An undeniable reality of being human is that pain and suffering are inevitable. We all hurt. We all suffer. We all experience loss and grief. Some hurt more than others but there is simply no way to avoid it. The most difficult part of any minister's job is helping people work through their pain. Divorce, addiction, depression, loneliness, infidelity, financial hardship, fear, worry, and relentless anxiety are all real problems in our complicated world. Thich Nhat Hanh has a new book called *The Art of Living* in which he says, "Many of us want to do something to help the world suffer less. We see so much violence, poverty, and environmental destruction all around us. But if we are not peaceful, if we don't have enough compassion, then we can't do much to help. We ourselves are the center. We have to make peace and reduce the suffering in ourselves first because we represent the world. Peace, compassion, and well-being begin with ourselves." This is a truth that many overlook.

Jesus commands us to "love others as we love ourselves," and I am convinced that many people are doing that. They are hurting others because they are hurting inside themselves. It is a vicious and dangerous cycle. It's only when we first tend to our own soul and healing that we can then tend to others. Most of the time when people lash out in anger, there is something going on inside. They are simply projecting the way that they are feeling. Hurting people will hurt others. But the question still remains: how do we grow through our pain? How does it change us? How does it make us stronger? With every challenge of life comes a new opportunity for growth.

13. Overcoming Life's Disappointments

Rabbi Harold Kushner wrote a book back in 2006 entitled *Overcoming Life's Disappointments*. It's a great book built around the story of Moses. Kushner says that if you think about it, Moses is a pivotal figure in the Old Testament, and there is a lot that we can learn from his life—particularly from the many disappointments that he had to face. Moses is called by God to lead the Israelites out of Egypt only to find Pharaoh being stubborn, uncooperative, and unwilling to compromise. After a series of plagues that God sends on the Egyptian people, Moses is able to finally lead the Israelites out of Egypt. Once they get into the desert, rather than being thankful that they have been freed from slavery and from Pharaoh's rule, they start complaining that they have nothing to eat and nothing to drink. In fact, they wish that they were back in slavery in Egypt where at least they were fed. You could say that Moses's life was one of a man who remained faithful to God despite the ongoing disappointments and let downs. He had to persevere and press on despite all the setback and inconveniences. Kushner concludes his first chapter by saying, "What if we could be like Moses in our ability to overcome disappointments, frustrations, and the denial of our dreams? What if we could learn from Moses how to respond to disappointment with faith in ourselves and in our future and to respond to heartbreak with wisdom instead of bitterness and depression? Can Moses teach us how to be ourselves, our best selves, even when life doesn't turn out as we had hoped it would? "The answer," Kushner says, "is yes."

If you stop and think about the disappointments that we all face in life, most of them fall within three categories.

The first has to do with relationships. We get disappointed at an early age in life when we learn that people will let us down. We get our hearts broken. We pour out our feelings for somebody and then find out they don't feel the same way. We want to become friends with someone, but that person doesn't return the friendship. Marriages don't work out, and people who never thought they'd be divorced end up getting divorced. Or people that go into a marriage thinking everything will be perfect find out that marriage is not perfect. It takes work and effort at every stage of the game. Children disappoint their parents with the decisions they make. At later stages of life, children get disappointed by their parents when they discover that they are not perfect and that they have flaws and shortcomings.

Secondly, we can get disappointed when it comes to money and success. Some people feel like they should be further along their career path than they are. They think that they deserve to make more money than they do. Some people are very unfulfilled in their jobs, so they just go through the motions every day to make a living. They look around and see what everybody else has accumulated and then wonder why they can't have the same thing. They feel like they are missing out and that everybody else is better off. And for some reason we always tend to compare ourselves with people who have more and not with people who have less. Why is that?

The third category where we can get disappointed in life is with our health. We see pictures of ourselves from when we were younger and trimmer and we wonder, "What happened? Why can't I look like that anymore?" It's hard to keep weight off, our bodies start to ache and give out on us, and we get frustrated. Then, we begin to face medical problems—

some that we can control, others that we can't. Some of us have to take care of our parents because they are getting up there in years, and that certainly takes a lot of our time and energy. Our health, both physical and mental, becomes something that we have to constantly monitor and work on, and it can become something that constantly frustrates and disappoints us.

The bottom line is—anybody who lives life faces disappointment. Some experience more disappointment than others, but all of us experience it. So again, the question is not "Do we experience disappointment in life," the question is "How do we deal with it, and how do we overcome it?" At the end of the book, Rabbi Kushner says, "If you have been brave enough to love, and sometimes you won and sometimes you lost; if you have cared enough to try, and sometimes it worked and sometimes it didn't; if you have been bold enough to dream with some that come true and some that don't—then you, like Moses, can realize how full your life has been and how richly you are blessed."

14. Why Do Bad Things Happen?

Theologians have been wrestling with the question of "theodicy" since the beginning of time. Simply put, if God is all powerful and all loving, then why do bad things happen in life? This question has caused many to turn from their faith. The truth is, we never get an answer that completely satisfies us. Rob Bell gives his understanding of pain and suffering in his book *Love Wins*. Bell says this: "Love demands freedom. It always has, and it always will. Love, by its very nature, is freedom. For there to be love, there has to be the option to not love. To turn the other way. To reject the love extended. To say no. Although God is powerful and mighty, when it comes to the human heart God has to play by the same rules we do. God has to respect our freedom to choose to the very end, even at the risk of the relationship itself. If at any point, God overrides, co-opts or hijacks the human heart, robbing us of our freedom to choose, then God has violated the fundamental essence of what love even is."

In life, we cannot have love without freedom and choice. And we cannot have love without the risk of loss and hurt. We ask the questions, "Why? Why do we have to go through some of the things that we do? Why we have to suffer? Why we have to hurt? Why we have to say good bye to those we love?" As we try to answer these questions, we must acknowledge that so many of these things are simply the result of being able to live and love. And love does not control. Love always brings risk. Whoever said that life is supposed to be perfect? It's just not.

Bell makes the point that, "People choose to live in their own hells all the time. We do it every time we isolate ourselves, give the cold shoulder to someone who has slighted us, every time we hide knives in our words, every time we harden our hearts in defiance of what we know to be the loving, good, and right thing to do." He says, "If we want isolation, despair, and the right to be our own god, God graciously grants us that option. If we insist on using our God-given power and strength to make the world in our own image, God allows us that freedom. If we want nothing to do with light, hope, love, grace, and peace, God respects that desire on our part, and we are given a life free from any of those realities…if we want nothing to do with love, we are given a reality free from love."

I believe that we are here for a purpose - to love and to be loved. That's what Jesus said. "Love the lord your God with all your heart, soul, mind, and strength, and love your neighbor as yourself." God has given each and every one of us the ability to be resilient, the ability to bounce back when terrible things happen. This is part of what I think it means to believe in the spirit of resurrection. New beginnings are always available—today and every day. That is what grace is all about. That's what forgiveness is all about. God gives us second chances, and third chances, and fourth chances, and God calls to do the same for each other. We should not live our lives expecting everything to be perfect and pain free. But we can live our lives knowing we have been put here to love, even when it hurts.

15. Good News for Broken People

It has become abundantly clear to me that there is a lot of shame in our culture. People are ashamed of things they have done in their past. They are ashamed of things that are going on in their lives. They are ashamed or embarrassed of situations their family members are facing. They are ashamed of things that they are struggling with. The church is supposed to be a "hospital for sinners, not a hotel for saints," yet there are still many people who think that you have to have everything in order to come and be a part of the church (especially a pretty church with a tall steeple sitting in the middle of Green Hills).

We put on our suits and our dresses. We get the kids dressed up. We put on our Sunday smiles. When people ask us how we are doing, we say, "Great, great...everything is great." But beneath the surface, there is brokenness. There is pain. There is suspicion. There is hurt. There is grief. There are scars. And then if you throw judgment on top of all of that, well... it's simply more than we can take. For example, if you've been through a divorce, you've probably already been to hell and back. If you've battled with an addiction, you've already struggled enough. And if you show up at the church and get judged or shunned for it, well that's not what you needed, and it only makes it worse. And so many people just stay away. And the community of faith where they are supposed to find love, support, and acceptance becomes something that they avoid at all costs. This is a serious challenge for the church as it moves into the future. One of the most genuinely honest gatherings in our society takes place at 12 step meetings—where people are honest with each other and they can be themselves. Where they say, "Hi, I'm John, and I'm an alcoholic."

A big part of my calling as a minister is to help people deal with the hurt, pain, and struggle that they experience in their lives. To make some sense of it. To persevere through it. To grow from it. To do what Paul says and realize that "suffering produces endurance, endurance produces character, character produces hope, and hope does not disappoint." As long as we have hope, we can press on.

No matter what happens to us in life, we need to hear the words of Paul, "I am convinced that neither death nor life, nor angels nor rulers, nor things present nor things to come, nor powers, nor height nor depth nor anything else in all creation can separate us from the love of God in Christ Jesus our Lord." This is what our world longs to hear. I've always had a problem with people who try to sort out who's going to heaven and whose not. It's not because I don't think their faith is genuine, but it's because it's not their call to make. It's God's call. Yet there are a lot of people who feel the need to make that call for whatever reason. I think we will all have to be accountable one day for how we have lived our lives, how we have treated other people, and how we have acted. But I still think that when it comes to deciding who is going to heaven, that's God's call. God is the judge, not us.

I think salvation is a life-long process. The "once saved always saved" phenomena doesn't really do it for me because I've met too many people who say they are "saved" yet they live a life that seems to indicate otherwise. Salvation is a gift from God through Christ that we call grace. And we respond to that gift by having faith. We don't deserve it or earn it, it's freely given. And like Paul, we should be convinced that no matter what may happen in life, no matter what we may be going through, no matter how hopeless a situation may feel—"neither death nor life, nor angels nor rulers, nor things present nor things to come, nor powers, nor height nor depth nor anything else in all creation can separate us from the love of God in Christ Jesus our Lord." That's the good news. So let us hear it. Let us receive it. Let us spread it. Let us live in the spirit and hope of it.

16. How Will You Measure Your Life?

I recently read a book by a professor at Harvard named Clayton Christensen. The book is titled, *How Will You Measure Your Life?* Back in 2010, Christensen gave a very moving speech to the graduating class of Harvard Business School. At the time, he had just overcome the same type of cancer that took his father's life, and so in addition to his ground-breaking research on innovation for which he is widely known, this book deals with other types of question such as: "How can I find satisfaction in my career? How can I be sure that my personal relationships become enduring sources of happiness? How can I avoid compromising my integrity as I climb the ladder of success?"

This question, "How will I measure my life" is one that we all think about each and every day, and it's a very important question. What does success look like? What does happiness look like? What do healthy relationships looks like? Many people suffer from "restless heart syndrome," which is the idea that we are never satisfied, we never have enough, and life always seems incomplete.

It's no secret that our world seems to measure success in certain ways: by money, possessions, fame, prestige, power, and influence. One of the things that Christensen talks about in his book is that when he would go back to Harvard for reunions of his own business school class, he noticed that lots of people were achieving success by the world's standards—earning large salaries, becoming CEO's of companies, gaining lots of influence and status. But the problem he saw was that many of them were having serious problems in their personal lives. They were losing their marriages. They had been through multiple divorces. They had no relationship with their children. And the only friends they had were superficial. And so he talks about this. That's why he asks the question, "How will you measure your life?" Because there are different ways for us to measure our lives.

Jesus had a lot to say about how we measure our lives, and many of his words are incredibly challenging. In fact, they stand in direct contrast to what the world says. In Luke 12, he says, "Be on guard against all types of greed. For one's life does not consist in the abundance of possessions." And in life, I have found that lots of people don't realize when they are being greedy. In Matthew 16, he says: "Those who want to save their life will lose it. And those who lose their life for my sake and for the sake of the gospel will find it. What will it profit them to gain the whole world and forfeit their life?" In other words, we find our lives by giving and helping others. And then in John's gospel, Jesus says this to his disciples in John 13: "I give you a new commandment, that you love one another. Just as I have loved you, you also should love one another. By this everyone will know you are my disciples, if you have love for one another." In the Sermon on the Mount, Jesus also said, "Do unto others as you would have them do unto you."

How will we measure our lives when it's all said and done? How can we live our lives so that we have few regrets at the end? These are question worth asking and answering no matter what stage we might be in.

17. How Will We Be Remembered?

Memorial Day weekend is a time to remember those who gave their lives in service and sacrifice to our nation as well as loved ones who have passed on before us. The free nation in which we live, despite its flaws and imperfections, has been made possible by the willing sacrifice of many who have gone before us. It might serve us well this weekend to ask the question, "How do we want to be remembered? What will our own legacy be?" More specifically, in the words of David Brooks, "Toward what should I orient my life? Who am I, and what is my nature? How do I mold my nature to make it gradually better day by day? What virtues are the most important to cultivate, and what weaknesses should I fear the most? How can I raise my children with a true sense of who they are and a practical set of ideas about how to travel along the road to character?"

In 1997, Father Thomas Keating gave a fascinating lecture at Harvard Divinity School titled, "The Human Condition." He said this: "We spend the first part of our lives finding a role—becoming a mother or father, a professor, a doctor, a minister, a soldier, a business person, an artisan, or whatever. Whoever we think we are, we are not. We have to find that out and the best way to find that out, or at least the most painless way, is through the process that we call the spiritual journey. This requires facing the dark side of our personality and the emotional investment we have made in false programs for happiness and in our particular cultural conditioning." Of course, owning our character flaws and the darker side of our personality is not easy. Hubris always gets in the way. A desire to achieve and hide weakness will get in the way. But wrestling with our flaws and striving to become better is always a worthwhile endeavor. Clayton Christiansen says, "The only metrics that will truly matter to my life are the individuals whom I have been able to help, one by one, to become better people." Our culture is very self-centered, fast-paced, and anxiety-filled. This has made spiritual growth more difficult yet more necessary than ever before. There are certain virtues we should all strive to embrace—faith, hope, peace, joy, kindness, patience, and compassion. Each of the great religions teaches these things. There are also traits that should be avoided—cynicism, pessimism, negativity, anger, envy, and selfishness. But there is one virtue greater than all the others, transcending all the others, and that is love. Love is the most powerful force on earth. It has the potential to heal and redeem a broken world, but it must be put into practice. In the homily that he gave at the royal wedding last weekend, Bishop Michael Curry said this before a global audience: "There's power in love. There's power in love to help and heal when nothing else can. There's power in love to lift up and liberate when nothing else will. There's power in love to show us the way to live. Set me as a seal on your heart... a seal on your arm, for love is as strong as death." When it's all said and done, what matters most is that we discovered how to love, and we let others love us.

18. Reflections of a Suicide Survivor

A number of recent studies indicate that suicide levels are at an all-time high. Some of these studies show that suicide is also becoming more and more common among young people. Suicide has been defined before as "a permanent fix to a temporary problem." However, it may not be that simple. I lost my mother to suicide eleven years ago. Rarely does a day go by when I don't think about her and all the life she missed out on—weddings, grandchildren, birthdays, friendships, etc. She had a long battle with severe depression which led to a state of utter hopelessness. Many people that make the decision to take their own lives are in a very dark place. Many are ill, suffering from a mental condition that renders them incapable of enjoying life the way others enjoy life. They simply want the pain to stop and to go away. Many feel like they won't be missed, and the world would be just fine without them. Thankfully these illnesses are becoming less stigmatized in our culture, and people can seek the help they need through counseling and medication. More times than not, depression results from a chemical imbalance in the brain.

In regard to depression, Harvard psychiatrist Armand Nicholi Jr. once remarked, "The cause of despondency in many today is an awareness of a gap between what they think they ought to be and what they feel they are. There is a discrepancy between an ideal they hold for themselves and an acute awareness of how far short they fall from the ideal." Society must play a role in helping people find hope and meaning. Social isolation has become a major problem, and digital screens are a pathetic substitute for authentic community and connection. Young people need to know that they are loved, supported, and treasured. They don't have to handle all the challenges of life alone. Parents need to communicate with them openly and often. Counselors will tell you that fear and anxiety are at an all-time high, leading many to feel completely overwhelmed and discouraged. Social psychologist Jonathan Haidt says that real happiness does not come from getting or achieving; it does not come from within, but it comes from meaningful connections with others because we are social creatures. Therefore, those who work towards developing meaningful relationships in life seem to be more satisfied and fulfilled. We were not designed to live in isolation so we must work diligently to remain connected to each other.

As humans we all wrestle with the same challenges, the same stresses, and the same fears, so we must learn to share them with each other and draw support from each other. Nobody has to live alone even when feelings of utter isolation and helplessness lead to despair and emptiness. There is no need to judge those who have taken their own lives for whatever reason. The only need we have is to build a world where people don't feel isolated and helpless, as if they are shouldering life's burdens by themselves. Reach out to those who are hurting. Let them know they are not alone. Pay close attention to those around you because somebody you love dearly may be struggling in ways you might never imagine.

19. Our Search for Meaning

My wife and I just welcomed our third child into the world. At the hospital, there were all kinds of babies—red, yellow, black, and white—all precious in God's sight. Becoming a parent again causes me to ask: "What kind of world is he being born into? What does the future have in store? Socrates once said, "The unexamined life is not worth living." How often do we pause and ask, "What is the meaning and purpose of life. What are we supposed to be doing?" Many answers are given: To love and to be loved; to make the world better than you found it, to serve others; to commune with God; to create peace; to live in the present; to be content and grateful; to help others with their pain; to bring God's kingdom to earth; to serve others; to give back; to forgive and be forgiven; to grow in knowledge and wisdom; to form meaningful relationships; to love God and neighbor. How would you answer this very important question? Even as our family is experiencing great joy at this time, there are many who are hurting. Racial tension remains high. Lives have been taken for senseless reasons. Politics are polarizing. Social isolation is real. Many can't pay the bills and feel inadequate. As a minister, I often become overwhelmed by the amount of pain and hurt in life. Illness, cancer, addiction, loss, divorce, grief, loneliness, racism, violence, unemployment—it's all there. When we don't deal with our own pain, we then go and hurt others, and it becomes a terrible cycle.

Victor Frankl, who survived the Nazi concentration camp at Auschwitz, wrote the classic book called *Man's Search for Meaning*. In the book, he makes a few timeless claims. The first is, "We can survive the HOW in life as long as we know the WHY." The second is this: Even if we lose everything in life, there is one thing that cannot be taken away from us, and that is our ability to choose our attitude in any given circumstance. Ecclesiastes reminds us that many of the things we chase after in search of meaning and happiness are futile and don't deliver. Humans are notorious for turning to the wrong things seeking fulfilment and security. It's a superficial world. All great religions recognize this. Only life in God can give us meaning. Only deeper connections with others will last. St. Augustine said, "Lord you have made us for yourselves, and our heart is restless until it finds its rest in you." Restlessness keeps us from being present. Worry and fear keep us on edge. Prayer makes a difference. Life is a series of ups and downs, joys and sorrows, victories and defeats, jubilation and heartbreak. As human beings, we can't even begin to make sense of and comprehend it all. The universe is vast. Our minds are limited. And we are complicated creatures with the ability to inflict hurt on each other. Friends come and go and everything changes. How then shall we live? Tim McGraw offers significant wisdom in his recent song, "Always stay humble and kind." Thankfully, we get to journey together, trusting in God, searching for God, giving thanks, loving others, and knowing that we are never alone.

20. Two Ways of Living

As we begin the transition from Thanksgiving to the Christmas Season and all of the hustle and bustle that the holidays bring, it occurs to me that there are two basic ways to approach life (and shades of each). The first is the way of fear, and it could be called an "ontologically disappointed life." With this approach, life is a burden, people always let you down, nothing is ever good enough, and life is unfair. This approach is grounded in cynicism, negativity, pessimism, and disappointment. Fear becomes the dominating emotion, and anxiety rules the day. There is always somebody out to get you, screw you over, hurt you, or take what you have. With this approach, you never get the credit or recognition you deserve. You take blessings for granted, develop a sense of entitlement, and complain often that things aren't as they should be. People who live this way are rarely happy, satisfied, fulfilled, or content. They are very good at playing the victim and any type of change is viewed as a threat. These individuals are often miserable.

The second way of living is the healthier way: the way of hope and love. With this approach, life is an exciting adventure. Others do not control you. Joy is found in the small things. Nothing is taken for granted, and every day is viewed as a gift and an opportunity. You don't get bogged down with the past or become obsessed over the future. People who live this way learn to count their blessings on a daily basis and thanksgiving becomes a way of being. These individuals live the Advent virtues of hope, peace, joy, and love. The fruits of the spirit become the goal—including patience, kindness, gentleness, generosity, and self-control. This approach tries to make the most of any situation and does not complain about circumstances. This approach involves a healthy recognition that many things are out of our control, and that is perfectly okay. This second approach to life is one that generates warmth, compassion, and a sense of authenticity. Fear is kept in check. Intentional steps are taken to reduce anxiety and stress. Experiencing inner peace becomes very important. These are individuals who move beyond narcissism and selfishness so that they can learn to live for others. Serving and giving back become a way of life.

You could call the second approach the "road less traveled." These two ways of living life, fear versus love, ultimately boil down to a choice, and we all get to make that choice on a daily basis. Concentration camp survivor Victor Frankl once concluded that we don't always control our circumstances, but we do get to control how we will respond to our circumstances. That simply cannot be taken away from us. Clearly, the second approach is a healthier way to live, but many people don't choose it. The Christmas Season is a time of "peace on earth, goodwill to all," and it's the perfect time to choose the second approach to life. After all, nobody is promised or guaranteed tomorrow. All we have is today.

21. Words for Living

How can we live a life of humility? How can we heed the words of the Prophet Micah and "walk humbly with God?" How can we keep from maintaining an overly exalted opinion of ourselves in an age of competition, egos, rugged individualism, and self-righteousness? There are many different ways, but there are three phrases that I think we should all learn to use more and more.

First of all, we should not be afraid to say, "I'M WRONG." Oh, how we hate to say those words. We feel humiliated, ashamed, embarrassed, weak, and vulnerable. Yet being able to admit when we are wrong in life is one of the most important things that we can ever do because we are not always right. There was a book published in 2010 by Kathryn Shulz titled *On Being Wrong: Adventures in the Margin of Error*. Drew Faust, who is now serving as the 28th President of Harvard University once said that if there is one book she would recommend to her students, it would be this one. In that book, Schulz says, "To err is to wander and wandering is the way we discover the world and lost in thought it is also the way we discover ourselves. Being right might be gratifying but in the end it is static a mere statement. Being wrong is hard and humbling and sometimes even dangerous but in the end it is a journey and a story." How can we ever learn anything in life if we are always right? It is impossible to always be right. And nobody wants to be around somebody who thinks that they are always right. That gets old very quickly. Tony Jarvis says, "How hard it is to say, 'I was wrong.' How tempting it is to make artful excuses, to pass the buck to someone else or to some force beyond our control. How tempting it is to lie, and obfuscate, and evade. How terribly hard it is to face up and say, 'I'm wrong.'" Learning to say "I'm wrong" is a big part of what it means to be humble.

Secondly, we should learn to say, "I'm sorry" more often. I'm sorry for hurting you. I'm sorry for being cruel to you. I'm sorry for not understanding you. I'm sorry for not being there to help you. Saying "I'm sorry" shows strength, and not weakness. Saying "I'm sorry" is a big part of what it means to be humble. We all make mistakes. We all overreact. We all treat people badly from time to time. We all do things that we regret. I would even say it is impossible to have healthy relationships in life if we are not willing to say we are sorry. Nothing is more destructive in relationships than refusing to be vulnerable. Love means learning to say "I'm sorry" more often and really mean it. Marriages would be stronger if we would apologize more often. Business relationship would be better. Friendships would be closer. There is something very profound in learning to say "I 'm sorry," even if we don't understand what we did to hurt somebody.

Thirdly, the final phrase we should learn to use in life is "Please help me." We don't like to ask for help because we think it shows weakness. We think it shows incompetence and insecurity. Part of being spiritual and having faith is learning to be still and to turn our worries and cares over to God, to trust God with the things that trouble us the most, and then to let those things go. And we must learn that there are simply times in life when we need to ask for help.

About a year ago, a friend of mine who had been through a rough time gave me a book by Andrew Murray because it had had a tremendous impact on his life. Murray was Christian writer and pastor who lived in South Africa. But this particular book is entitled *Humility*, and this is what Murray says: "Humility is perfect quietness of heart. It is for me to have no trouble; never to be fretted or vexed or irritated or sore or disappointed. It is to expect nothing, to wonder at nothing that is done to me, to feel nothing done against me. It is to be at rest when nobody praises me and when I am blamed or despised. It is to have a blessed home in the Lord where I can go in and shut the door and kneel to my Father in secret and be at peace as in a deep sea of calmness when all around is trouble." The more often we can use these three phrases, the more humble we will become.

II

VALUES

22. Essential Foundations for Healthy Relationships

Relationships matter in life, but they are complicated. They are the source of great joy, happiness, and fulfillment as well as great pain, heartache, and disappointment. Everybody experiences both. We recently returned from a family trip to Virginia where we celebrated the 50th wedding anniversary of my wife's parents. They were college sweethearts at Depauw University and got married after graduation at age twenty-two back in 1968. It was a joy to celebrate with them and to see how their love has grown and deepened over the years. Unfortunately, fifty year wedding anniversaries are not as common as they used to be. People are now getting married later in life, and the divorce rate remains over fifty percent. Dr. John Gotttman says that the only empirical evidence in his research between couples whose marriage lasts over the years and the ones that don't boils down to this: does the couple learn to honor and respect the friendship? It's much more challenging than it sounds. We must work to avoid criticism, defensiveness, contempt, and stonewalling, all of which lead to problems. In his book *Wisdom: Life's Great Treasure*, Richard E. Simmons offers the following insight for being intentional in marriage:

1. Do not be afraid to go for counseling. Counseling is healthy.
2. Set aside time to be alone with your spouse, particularly when you are raising your children. This has to be planned. Many couples have arranged consistent date nights. Anniversary trips are important and meaningful.
3. See the wisdom of couples who are further down the road

in their marriages than you. This can be incredibly helpful.

4. Read good books on marriage. (*Sacred Marriage* by Gary Thomas, *Five Love Languages* by Gary Chapman, *The Meaning of Marriage* by Tim Keller).

In American culture, we often define ourselves by our profession: lawyer, doctor, banker, minister, teacher, therapist. Perhaps we need to put as much of an emphasis on the other roles we play: husband, wife, father, mother, sister, brother, son, daughter. These are the roles that matter most in the big picture. Marriage is hard but also very rewarding. There are reasons why many marriages don't make it, and those who suffer through a divorce should not be judged but picked up because they've been through a lot. There are some basic foundations upon which healthy relationships and marriages must be based: honesty, trust, selflessness, sacrifice, compromise, patience, and forgiveness. Falling in love is easy. Staying in love takes work. Gary Thomas says, "I have a theory, behind virtually every case of marital dissatisfaction lies an unwillingness to admit our self-centeredness. Couples do not fall out of love so much as they are unwilling to humbly acknowledge they have shortcomings as a spouse. Sin, wrong attitude, and unresolved personal failures slowly erode the relationship." It is not surprising that as our culture becomes more self-centered, more and more relationships struggle. Building relationships and marriage on the right foundations will help ensure stability and longevity for the future.

23. Taking Off Our Masks

Today is Halloween, and both children and adults will enjoy the thrill of putting on costumes and masks, a temporary escape from reality. However, we can recognize that it doesn't take Halloween for people in our culture to pretend to be somebody that they are not. All of us, no matter who we are, find ourselves in many different roles (i.e. minister, husband, father, son), wearing multiple hats. But the challenge is to be the same person no matter which role we might be in. To act the same way. To treat others the same way. To not put on a front just because we are going to be around new people, important people, rich people, or church people.

We live in a superficial world where people have mastered putting up fronts. Everything is judged on the surface. We wear masks. There is a lack of depth. People who are hurting put a smile on their faces and pretend that everything is alright. People who are scared to death act like they are courageous and pretend that they are being brave. People who have lost their jobs and their savings try to continue living their same lifestyles so that others won't catch on to the fact that their bank accounts have dwindled, and they are not doing well at all. People whose marriages are struggling act happy and pretend like everything is fine when in actuality, they cry themselves to sleep at night. It's also a world of people pleasing. Many aren't true to themselves because they're too busy living out somebody else's expectations. They want to please their spouses, their parents, their in-laws, their children, or their friends, so they spend all of their time doing things that they think will please other people rather than being honest and true to who they really are.

And why do we do these things? We do these things because we feel like society expects us to be somebody that we're not, and we're scared of being discovered. We're scared that others might discover who we really are and then decide that they want nothing to do with us. We're scared that if we let down our guard, then others may not let down theirs and we'll look like the only person that has problems. But we all have problems. We all have shortcomings and character flaws. We are well-aware of the things that we do that we wish we didn't do: worry, act of jealousy, lust, anger, bitterness, envy, resentment, or fear. We overreact to certain situations. We say things about people that we shouldn't and if it comes back to us, we deny it. We put on fronts, smiles, and pretend to live a problem free life, but nobody has a problem free life.

We all have one thing in common as humans—we are broken to some degree. The Bible calls this sin. But the good news is that God's grace is available to each of us in the midst of our brokenness—all we have to do is accept it through faith. We don't have to wear masks. We don't have to pretend to be somebody we're not. We don't have to pretend. We can be our true selves every day. Authenticity is liberating.

24. Beyond Narcissism

The DSM IV, stands for the *Diagnostic and Statistical Manual of Mental Disorders—Fourth Edition.* It is used by almost every psychologist, psychiatrist, and physician when diagnosing mental disorders in a clinical setting. Late last year, it was announced that the DSM V, scheduled to come out in 2013, would not include Narcissistic Personality Disorder as one of its classifications. Many feel this disorder is being left out because there are just too many people in our culture that now fit into this category. Recently, this has caused quite a stir in the world of psychology. There was even one headline that read: "A fate narcissists will hate - being ignored!" The central requirement for Narcissistic Personality Disorder is a special kind of self-absorption: a grandiose sense of self, a serious miscalculation of one's abilities and potential that is often accompanied by fantasies of greatness. To put it in layman's terms, narcissists think that the world revolves around them—that they are the center of everything. And because we now live in an age where far too many people meet these criteria, the disorder will be left out of this very important clinical manual. Now take just a moment and think about what this is saying about our society: we are way too self-absorbed.

Throughout his life and ministry, Jesus was constantly teaching his followers to think about others, to look out for others, to help others, to serve others, to forgive others, to love others, to have compassion for others, and to put others first. He says: "If any want to become my followers, let them deny themselves and take up their cross and follow me. For those who want to save their life will lose it. And those who lose their life for my sake will find it." These words sum up what Christianity is all about and tell us why being a Christian in today's world is hard. It's challenging. It's counter-cultural in many ways. We all know that we live in an age where we are taught to take care of ourselves, to look out for ourselves, to do well for ourselves, and most of the decisions that people make are in their own best interest. So we hear these words of Jesus about "denying self," and we're not quite sure what to make of it. We're not quite sure what to do about it.

In his book *With Love and Prayers,* former Roxbury Latin headmaster Tony Jarvis has a chapter entitled "Beyond Self Absorption," and in it he says, "Life involves a continual temptation to return to self-absorption." He says, "There is a great tendency in all of us to withdraw into ourselves, or into safe little cliques of like-minded people—to live sheltered, claustrophobic, risk-free, boring little lives." This is often our natural inclination as human beings. But Jarvis goes on to say that the Christian faith "calls us to involve ourselves in the lives of other people. It calls us to go against our natural, innate tendencies of self-absorption. It calls us to care. It calls us not just to tolerate, not just to involve ourselves, but to actually love one another. Self-absorption, when it's all said and done—brings about unhappiness. Happiness, on the other hand, only comes from self-risk, inconvenient involvement, self-sacrifice, and love." Selfish and narcissistic people are usually not very happy people.

The Christian life is one that is completely dedicated to following our leader—Jesus Christ—in all that we say and in all that we do. We are not committed to a preacher or a church or a political party or a cause but to Christ. I often worry that both churches and Christians are so easily sidetracked and distracted by so many things—social issues that cause division, politics, materialism, status, busy schedules, conflict, you name it. And what happens is Christianity becomes a religion of convenience. It becomes a religion that just fills in the gaps when we don't have something else planned.

Jesus says, "Follow me," and that doesn't mean follow me some of the time, or follow me when you feel like it, or follow me when you've got nothing else to do on Sunday morning, but follow me all the time. It is possible for a person to gain everything by the standards of this world—and then to wake up one morning completely empty and unsatisfied, completely lost and unfulfilled. It happens all the time. Self-denial is difficult but always worthwhile.

25. Does Character Still Matter?

Of the many question remaining after 2017, there is one that seems clear: does character still matter in this culture? The sexual harassment scandals that have brought down many powerful men in multiple industries point to a problem that has been overlooked and dismissed in our culture for far too long. At the Golden Globe Awards on Sunday night, Oprah Winfrey said, "For too long, women have not been heard or believed if they dare speak truth to the power of those men. But their time is up. Their time is up." 2017 opened our eyes to something that has been going on for a long time, and it needs to stop.

Harvey Weinstein, Matt Lauer, Charlie Rose, Roy Moore, Al Franken, and a host of other people now serve as examples of how you shouldn't behave. Many are quick to add Bill Clinton and Donald Trump to the mix. It is important to remember that these are the exceptions and not the norm. There are many good and decent men out there who do not treat women this way and never have. What exactly does it mean to have character? My mother once told me that "some people have character and some people are characters." I've never forgotten that. There are many rich and powerful people who feel like they get to play by a different set of rules. We all have weaknesses and flaws. The real struggle in life is learning to come to terms with those weaknesses and be committed to becoming a better person.

David Brooks concludes his book, *The Road to Character* by saying that, "The person who successfully struggles against weakness and sin may or may not become rich and famous, but that person will become mature." He says, "The mature person has moved from fragmentation to centeredness, has achieved a state in which the restlessness is over, the confusion about the meaning and purpose of life is calmed." That is quite a goal and I would argue that few people achieve it. The most important lessons we can learn are often the most obvious: the way we treat one another and the way we function together as a society matters. We should work to avoid certain things in our personal lives and interactions: selfishness, arrogance, condescension, hatred, anger, envy, bitterness, indifference, and resentment. We should work for the well-being of all. Humility matters. Words and tone matter. Confronting our fears and managing our anger matters. Most importantly, we must not be afraid to change, grow, live, and act differently. We must not be afraid to admit our shortcomings and work to become superior to our former selves. Everybody is a work in progress.

26. Digital Age Feeds Envy and Narcissism

It is obvious that technology has completely transformed and revolutionized our culture over the past few decades and social media is playing a major role in that process. There is no going back. True, we are connected with many people, but are those relationship authentic? Although information can be shared at lightning speed, is there now too much information? True, we have friends across the nation and globe, but do we still walk across the street to meet our neighbors? Have we stopped to consider the downside of a culture becoming more and more addicted to social media and social comparison? Specifically, I am talking about the growing level of narcissism, self-absorption, and envy in our culture. Narcissism has been defined as "a special kind of self-absorption: a grandiose sense of self, a serious miscalculation of one's abilities and potential that is often accompanied by fantasies of greatness." To put it in layman's terms, narcissists think that the world revolves around them—that they are the center of the universe. Enter Facebook, Twitter, and Instagram, and what do we have? Growing levels of social comparison and self-centered behavior. Look at me. Look at my house. Look at my children. Look at my new car. Look at our vacation. Look at what I'm making for dinner. And as you may have noticed, bad pictures are generally not posted. It's all glamorous. We live in a competitive culture and social media has now upped the ante.

I see some devastating spiritual consequences to growing self-preoccupation and constant social comparisons. Remember, it was Jesus who taught us to pay more attention to others but in a compassionate, loving, and not envious kind of way. He said, "Deny self, follow me, and love your neighbor as yourself." Overcoming selfishness, self-absorption, and envy is a worthy spiritual challenge for all of us. Will Willimon and Stanley Hauerwas once wrote a book titled *The Truth About God* (1999), and in referring to the ninth and tenth Commandments that deal with coveting, they talk about the spiritual challenges of a competitive culture. "What we want is power and status. Like the rich fool in Jesus' parable, we attempt to resist knowledge of our own insignificance by insulating ourselves with things. Alas, we find that no matter what we have acquired, there is always someone we envy." Why? Somebody else always has more. The grass always seems greener. There are obvious benefits to social media, but at the same time, it has become an unhealthy addiction for many resulting in a complete preoccupation with others, what they have, and what they are doing. Of course, not everybody on social media is narcissistic and jealous. But the general trend is to prove that we are important, significant, and affluent, and to do our best to keep up with everybody else. Like so many other things in life, the key is balance, taming desire, learning to count our blessings (privately), and be grateful for what we have. Gratitude reduces envy and anxiety.

27. Envy, Happiness, and Gratitude

The Thanksgiving season is an ideal time for us to acknowledge the fundamental difference between envy and gratitude, coveting and contentment. We seem to live in a culture with an economic system that, to some degree, fuels itself on coveting. Are we not told over and over again by marketers and advertisers that we deserve things that are bigger, better, and nicer than what we have? Are we not told that we would be so much happier if we just went out and bought whatever it is they are promoting because we deserve it? Isn't the American Dream predicated on the fundamental concept of having a better life than the previous generation? We don't just want to give our kids what we had—we want to give them something bigger and better, right? And then we wonder why we are never satisfied and why so many feel entitled.

There was a study done at Princeton asking the question, "What level of household income does it take in order to be happy?" They used Gallup data from roughly half a million Americans and here's what they discovered. The comfortable income standard for happiness in the United States is somewhere around $75,000. In other words, once a household income is above $75,000, they found that there is not much correlation to increased happiness. Clearly they forgot to survey the people of Green Hills for our input. Their argument is once you get above $75,000, your happiness level does not go up in proportion to your income. Sure, you might have a nicer car or a bigger house, but your basic needs are still being met. There was another study done at Harvard over a 75-year period. They tracked 268 male students who graduated from Harvard between the years of 1938 and 1940, men who are now well into their 90's, in order to find out what makes for a happy and meaningful life over the long haul. Guess what they discovered? Love is what matters most. Connection to other people and forming friendship is what matters. Moving from narcissism to connection is what matters, and working through challenges and adversity in life makes us who we are; without struggle, we cannot build character and learn resilience. They found that money and power, although important in achieving business success, do not necessarily equate to more happiness unless they are accompanied by the other things that bring us love, connection, and joy. Believe it or not, there are some lonely billionaires still looking for purpose.

Duke theologians Stanley Hauerwas and Will Willimon once said, "Our problem as humans is not that we are full of desire, aflame with unfulfillment. Our problem is that we long for that which is unfulfilling. We attempt to be content with that which can never satisfy…What we want is power and status. Alas, we find that no matter what we have acquired, there is always someone we envy." We should heed the words of Paul as we move towards Thanksgiving: "I have learned to be content with whatever I have. I know what it is to have little, and I know what it is to have plenty." Genuine gratitude for what we already have can help eliminate fear and anxiety, envy and jealousy.

28. The Liberating Power of Forgiveness

Forgiveness is one of those words that Christians throw around but often fail to practice. It's an age-old question: "Do we have to forget in order to truly forgive?" Is forgetting really possible? I would say that forgiveness is not contingent upon forgetting. We all have a memory, we know who has hurt us, and there are certain things that we would like to forget but can't. Some would say that if we can't forget a time when somebody has hurt us, then we really haven't forgiven them, but I'm not sure that is necessarily true. Just because we have forgiven somebody does not mean that we should put ourselves in the place to be hurt again. You've heard that old saying, "Hurt me once, shame on you…hurt me twice, shame on me." I think it is possible to forgive others and then keep a safe distance. We can protect ourselves from being hurt again because that is the wise and logical thing to do. But remember, Jesus said that there should never be a limit in terms of the number of times that we forgive another person. Now this gets a little bit more difficult when it comes to marriage and family. Part of the reason why there are rifts in families is because somebody has been hurt, there may be forgiveness, but still you don't really feel close again. You don't really feel like things have been restored to the way they once were. And when it comes to marriage and family, there is always the chance that they could hurt you again once you have forgiven them. And if you want to be close to somebody, you have to take that chance.

It's important to understand that forgiveness is liberating. When we learn to forgive others in life, not only is that a gift to them, but we take an enormous burden off of our own shoulders. Some people go through life never forgiving others, and because of that, they carry more weight and stress around than they should. When you hold grudges, harbor resentment, or keep bringing up the past, it is impossible to fully focus on the present and the future. All of us have things in our past that we would rather leave in the past. And guess what, that is a possibility. But first you have to make a decision to do that. First, you have to make a decision to turn it over to God and to let it go once and for all. And making the decision to forgive somebody may be a big part of that. Forgiveness is a choice, and until we make that choice to forgive, we will never be able to find peace in life because it will fester and grow inside of us. And whoever did us wrong and whoever has hurt us will continue to control and rule our lives. I realize that certain situations are not always that simple because people do some terrible things.

In life, we project so many of our problems onto other people because we have a hard time dealing with them ourselves. Forgiveness has liberating power in marriage, in friendships, in family, at work. If we truly practice forgiveness we can wipe the slate clean and begin anew. And the truth is—we all need it, therefore we must all practice it. Somebody once said, "Failing to forgive others and holding on to anger is like drinking a poison and expecting somebody else do die."

29. Living with Character and Values

Nashville lost a judicial and spiritual giant with the recent passing of Justice Frank F. Drowota III. Drowota moved to Nashville with his family when he was only five years old so his father could serve as the founding minister of Woodmont Christian Church. He was first elected to the Tennessee Supreme Court in 1980 as the youngest justice to ever hold that position. He served as Chief Justice of the Court two different times and retired in 2005 as the second longest serving justice in Tennessee history. Drowota's judicial accomplishments are well-documented, and his fingerprints are all over the law, but even more impressive than that are the personal and spiritual values he exhibited throughout his life. He was a man of faith, integrity, and learned about humility from his father.

Humility does not mean weakness; it is quiet strength. Humility is not thinking less of yourself, it is simply thinking of yourself less. Humility is in short supply in a world of arrogance and superficiality. Jesus was humble. Drowota was less interested in talking the talk and much more interested in walking the walk. The Bible Belt is full of people who are good at "talking Christian," but Drowota understood what St. Francis meant when he said, "Preach the gospel, and use words only when necessary." He was a true moderate and did not believe that any one side had a monopoly on the truth. He had the maturity to hear opposing viewpoints and not be threatened. The bitter partisanship and lack of civility in our culture troubled him, especially in recent years. Drowota kept his values in place: he loved his family, his friends, his church, and the community in which he lived. For him, sitting on the bench was an honor and privilege. He lived graciously, generously, and believed with all his heart that mercy always trumps judgment. He thought that Jesus' question was a good one to ask: "Why do you see the speck in your neighbor's eye but fail to recognize the log in your own eye?" He exemplified every fruit of the spirit that the Apostle Paul refers to in Galatians 5—love, joy, peace, patience, kindness, generosity, faithfulness, gentleness, and self-control.

Drowota always treated others the way he wanted to be treated. He knew that when it came to the spiritual life, there is no destination, only a life-long journey that is full of ups and downs, victories and defeats. Inner work is required, and self-reflection is necessary, so beware of those who feel they have arrived. He was wary of those who feel like they have all the answers because life is not that simple. There are nuanced positions that only emotionally mature people are able to sustain. Our society and world have many challenges, and we need more people like Judge Drowota. Harvard professor Clayton Christiansen asks the question, "How will you measure your life?" For Drowota, the answer was simple: faith, family, service, humility, friendship, loyalty, mercy, and civility. If we can strive to live this way, we will look back with very few regrets.

30. Searching for Purpose

There is a tragic opioid addiction in our nation right now, and it is claiming many lives. In his essay titled "American Carnage," Chris Caldwell writes, "Drug addiction used to be a ghetto thing. Now Oxycodone has joined shuttered factories and Donald Trump as a symbol of white working class desperation and fecklessness." The bottom line is, there are many in our culture who lack a sense of meaning and purpose, and they are doing whatever it takes to make the pain go away. The statistics are simply staggering, and the death toll keeps rising. That begs the question: "What does it mean to live life with a sense of purpose?" A few weeks ago at a leadership conference in Orlando, I heard John C. Maxwell give his three-fold definition of success. First, know your purpose. Second, grow to your maximum potential. Third, sow seeds that benefit others. If we stick with the first part of this definition, we cannot help but acknowledge that many people do not know their purpose or live their lives with a sense of purpose. And when you have no sense of purpose, meaninglessness and emptiness pervade. Addiction can easily fill the void. I have always wrestled with the question, "what motivates people?" What gives people drive? What gives us purpose? Because until we can answer that question, we are simply going through the motions, staying busy, and living lives without meaning.

Some think the purpose of life is to go and make as much money as you can.

Some think the purpose of life is to impress as many people as you can.

Some think the purpose of life is to make as many connections as you can.

Some think the purpose of life is to give your children things you didn't have.

I think the meaning and purpose of life is much deeper and much more profound than any of these things: We are here to love and to be loved. We are here to worship God and not false idols. We are here to put others before ourselves. We are here to build healthy relationships based on authenticity and trust. We are here to lift each other up when life beats us down. We are here to look out for those who have little or nothing. We are here to show mercy and compassion. We are here to practice forgiveness and grace. We are here to serve and to leave the world better than we found it. Rick Warren begins his famous book *The Purpose Driven Life* with a profound statement: "It's not about you." In a world that has become increasingly selfish, narcissistic, materialistic, and often shallow, should it be a surprise that opioid addiction is now out of control? We discover our meaning and purpose when we move beyond ourselves, when we look to the world to see how our passion and skill can address needs of others. Until we learn how to do this, meaningless, restlessness, and emptiness will carry the day.

31. Warning Signs in Relationships

It is true that the quality of our relationships helps determine the quality of our lives. Human beings are social creatures and we long for intimacy and connections with others. The absence of this in marriage can lead to major problems. Authentic relationships with God and others lies at the heart of all healthy religion. In the same way that physicians can identify physical symptoms that point to declining health, the same is true in our relationships. Drs. John and Julie Gottman are the co-founders of the Gottman Institute at the University of Washington in Seattle. Over the years, they have done extensive research at their "love lab" on marriage and relationship dynamics. Marriage and Family Therapists all over the world have turned to the Gottmans for guidance and insight. In their research, they have been able to identify four behavioral patterns that, when unaddressed, can lead to major problems in relationships: criticism, contempt, defensiveness, and stonewalling. These have been referred to as the "four horsemen of the apocalypse," and can become problematic on many levels.

"Criticism" of a spouse or partner is very different from offering a critique or complaint. Criticism is usually directed towards a person's character and is not well received. When criticism becomes pervasive, it causes the other person to feel assaulted, rejected, and hurt. Criticism often paves the way for the other three horsemen. The second horseman is "contempt." The Gottmans conclude that contempt is "fueled by long-simmering negative thoughts about the partner." This often happens in a passive aggressive manner and is usually done to get a rise out of the other person. Contempt is the result of a deep resentment or a grudge that builds over time. The Gottmans have discovered that contemptuous relationships actually can weaken the immune system and our ability to fight off infection. The third horseman is "defensiveness," which is often the natural result of the first two. When we feel attacked or accused, our natural reaction is to be defensive towards our partner. This may be understandable, but defensiveness has a negative effect in our relationships. This is often the way that we turn the tables and blame our partner for something that is most likely our own fault. The fourth and final horseman is "stonewalling." Stonewalling is what happens when one person shuts down and simply blocks out the other. It is a clear indication that one of the partners has "checked out." Stonewalling is usually a last resort and is utilized when the negativity of the first three horsemen becomes overbearing.

These four behavioral patterns should serve as warning signs in any relationship or marriage and they should not be ignored. The Gottmans do offer antidotes to each of these. Criticism should be replaced by a gentle start up where feelings are expressed in a positive manner. Contempt should be replaced by a culture of appreciation where gratitude and affirmation is expressed. Defensiveness should be replaced by taking responsibility and apologizing for any wrongdoing. It may just be the result of a lack of communication. When stonewalling occurs, that often signals that the partner needs some time alone to do something soothing and enjoyable. Different people require varying amounts of personal time. Relationships can be very complicated, and they take effort and intentionality. However, learning to identify and avoid these patterns of behavior will lead to stronger marriages, closer friendships, healthier family life, and ultimately a better society.

32. Wanting Just a Little Bit More

It takes courage for preachers to address the subject of greed. That is not a popular topic for a Sunday morning sermon. Greed is a problem in any capitalistic society. In Luke 12, Jesus said, "Take Care! Be on your guard against all types of greed. For one's life does not consist in the abundance of possessions." How well does that verse go over at an Ivy League business school full of ambitious MBA students? The problem with greed is that nobody thinks they are being greedy because there is always somebody who has more. It's always others who are greedy. Wealth seems relative.

Stanley Hauerwas has been on the forefront of Christian ethics for decades now. In 2001, *Time Magazine* named him one of America's most influential theologians, an honor that gave him mixed emotions. Hauerwas has never been afraid to speak his mind and he is best known for his stance as a pacifist. However, he has also written extensively about greed, desire, and the spiritual challenges of capitalism. In a 2010 article he wrote for *Religion and Ethics*, he says, "For surely if any one characteristic is to be associated with greed, it is the presumption that no matter how much we may have we need 'more.' We need more because we cannot be sure that what we have is secure. So the more we have the more we must have in order to secure what we have." Hauerwas is honest about the fact that many Christians say that God will provide, but we live as though security comes only through possessions and accumulation. He concludes the article by saying: "Greed is thus rightly called a deadly sin because it perverts the possibility of a proper human relation to the Creator, from whom we have received all that we need as gift. Greed presumes and

80

perpetuates a world of scarcity and want—a world in which there is never 'enough.' But a world shaped by scarcity is a world that cannot trust that God has given all that we need. Greed, in other words, prohibits faith. But the inverse is also true. For it is in the Christian celebration of the Eucharist that we have the prismatic act that makes possible our recognition that God has given us everything we need. The Eucharist not only is the proclamation of abundance, but it is the enactment of abundance. In the Eucharist we discover that we cannot use Christ up. In the Eucharist we discover that the more the body and blood of Christ is shared, the more there is to be shared. The Eucharist, therefore, is the way the Christian Church learns to understand why generosity rather than greed can and must shape our economic relations."

For Hauerwas, the Eucharist is a reminder for Christians that God has given us enough in Christ and we are called to resist greed and be a generous people. Generosity has always been a spiritual practice, a mark of discipleship. It takes practice, intentionality, and disciple. It's been said, "We make a living by what we get, but we make a life by what we give." How true that is. We should work hard to succeed. But no matter how much we have, we should not keep it all to ourselves. To do so is to suffocate our own spirit.

33. Whatever Happened to Humility?

We live in a society where pride, ego, and arrogance run rampant and where we constantly seek and thrive on the praise and affirmation of others. We want others to affirm us. We want others to like us. We want others to think fondly of us. We want to feel like we are important, that we matter. The dilemma that many of us face is this: How can we live in a world that worships achievement and success, accomplishment and prestige, money and power, yet maintain a strong sense of humility in the process? How can we work hard to get an education, a good job, take care of our families and loved ones, and remain humble in the process? This is a challenge for all.

I have always believed that there are two different types of pride. There is "healthy pride" and there is "unhealthy pride." Healthy pride means taking pride in our work, pride in our family, pride in our appearance, and pride in our service and achievements. Pride in our character and reputation. Pride in living a life of integrity. But unhealthy pride means feeling that we are God's gift to the world, better than others, and that we are indispensable. There is also a big difference between having self-confidence and being arrogant. Our world is full of people who lack self-confidence as well as people who are arrogant and feel superior. The goal is to be somewhere in the middle because both extremes are unhealthy. Humility is the way that we temper our sense of accomplishment and tame our sense of importance. Humility is a worthy goal and an admirable trait to possess.

C.S. Lewis once said: "Humility is not thinking less of yourself, it is thinking of yourself less."

Thomas Merton: "Pride makes us artificial and humility makes us real."

Earnest Hemingway: "There is nothing noble in being superior to your fellow man. True nobility is being superior to your former self."

Rick Warren: "You cannot exalt God and yourself at the same time."

For every single one of us, being human means struggling with this ongoing tension between pride and humility. And it's not just a one-time struggle. It is constant. The truth is, we never master it although some do it better than others. Arrogance is a turn off. It's a sure sign of insecurity. And it's also unchristian because Christ was humble—not arrogant. He did not exalt himself. He lived a humble life, he served others, and he died a humble death. So part of being a disciple is learning what it means to be humble. And being humble is not always easy, especially in a world that glorifies power, influence, affluence, and success. But humility remains a necessary goal. Andrew Murray once said, "Humility is perfect quietness of heart. It is for me to have no trouble; never to be fretted or vexed or irritated or sore or disappointed. It is to expect nothing, to wonder at nothing that is done to me, to feel nothing done against me. It is to be at rest when nobody praises me and when I am blamed or despised."

34. You Can't Lead on Empty

Last Sunday evening, I was surprised to hear of the sudden resignation of Pete Wilson as the senior pastor of Crosspoint Church. Since coming to Nashville in 2007, I have admired Pete for his charisma, creativity, and his ability to draw unchurched and dechurched people to Crosspoint. To be frank and honest, it's hard to compete with Crosspoint. Fourteen years ago, Pete set out to build a church "where everybody is welcome because nobody's perfect." That is not only admirable, but also it lies at the heart of the gospel. Too many people in our culture have been hurt and scarred by religion and their church experience. Pete never wanted that to be the case at Crosspoint, and he succeeded in that goal. Last Sunday, he stood before his congregation and bravely said, "Leaders who lead on empty don't lead well. I'm tired and I'm broken." Every minister in America can relate to that.

What Pete Wilson articulated is how many leaders often feel—lonely, tired, beat up, and in need of renewal. There must first be something in your own cup before you can pour it out to others. It's like the oxygen mask on the airplane: put yours on first before helping others. M. Scott Peck begins his famous book *The Road Less Traveled* with the following words: "Life is difficult. This is a great truth, one of the greatest truths. Once we truly see this truth, we can transcend it." If life is difficult, then we can safely say that leadership is really difficult. Leadership is not for the faint of heart. It takes passion, conviction, nerve, thick skin, and resilience. Pete Wilson has all of these traits. Tony Jarvis says this about leadership in his book *With Love and Prayers*: "Leaders are caught in a catch 22. If a leader is strong, undeterred by projection, blame, and calumny, he is then labeled as arrogant, authoritarian, dictatorial. If he sets aside his initiatives, goes with the way the wind is blowing, if he backs down at all, he is immediately labeled as 'weak' and 'a waffler.'" There are many in our culture who want to be leaders but aren't willing to pay the price. They don't know what it entails. Many want the recognition and prestige without the responsibility, the glory without the hard work. Jarvis adds that leadership is not an end unto itself; it takes courage, it always involves being criticized, and it is costly.

Perhaps the best book I have ever read on leadership is Edwin Friedman's *Failure of Nerve* where he says that leaders fail when they lose heart and give in to anxiety. Leaders fail when they lose nerve. In the case of Pete Wilson, he did not fail. He succeeded. But he had the wisdom to understand that you can't lead on empty. It never works. Bravo, Pete, on a job well done! You have changed lives, you have spread hope, and you have laid a foundation that will last for years and years to come!

35. Character Matters More than Money

Friedrich Nietzshe lived during the second half of the nineteenth century and was known as a pessimistic nihilist who was hostile to Christianity and morality. However, despite his many issues, he was very intelligent and once made a prediction that should haunt all western people of faith. Nietzsche famously said, "One day, money will replace God in Western culture." If we take a look around, for many people today, Nietzsche's prediction has proven true. Money is perhaps the number one source of idolatry. Some people are much more concerned about net worth than self-worth. Materialism, consumerism, and superficiality often rule the day. The rat race is one big competition to see who can acquire the biggest, shiniest, most expensive new toys. Those who have money and means are often admired and respected. Those who don't can be looked down upon, but there is a shallowness to it all that any honest person can see.

Jesus was aware of the dangers of a materialistic mindset, so he addressed it often throughout his ministry. He said, "You cannot serve both God and wealth." One always wins. He also raises a profound question that every generation should ask: "What does it profit you to gain the whole world, but forfeit your soul?" (Mark 8). Alternatively, we can reframe this question in more modern ways: What does it profit you to build a huge company if you lose your marriage in the process? What does it profit you to be a workaholic if you miss all your children's games and plays? What does it profit you to become a multi-millionaire if you have no true friends left in your life, only the hangers on? To be clear, there is nothing wrong with making money. We all must do it to survive. There is nothing wrong with being wealthy as long as your values are in place. But here's the question: How can we prevent our culture from becoming one where money matters more than character? Some might argue it's too late. This may be true for some, but not for most.

A price tag cannot be placed on character and integrity. There is incalculable value in things like telling the truth, being kind, remaining humble, listening to others, helping the poor, feeding the hungry, withholding judgment, mentoring the young, visiting the sick, forgiving those who have hurt you, and spreading peace to a hostile world. Socioeconomic status has absolutely no bearing on whether you can or can't do these things. Even capitalist icon Ayn Rand once said this: "Money is only a tool. It will take you wherever you wish, but it will not replace you as the driver." If we are the drivers, where are we going? What are we trying to accomplish? What matters in the big picture? The tension is: "How do we exist in a society where money is needed to survive but not let it become an idol?" Nobody ever said it was easy, and it will always be an ongoing challenge. Winston Churchill famously said, "We make a living by what we get but we make a life by what we give." What kind of life are we making? What kind of priorities have we established? How do we differentiate between generosity and greed, self-absorption, and selflessness? Issues of character should always trump possessions. Or as scripture says: "Mortals look on the outward appearance, but the Lord looks on the heart."

36. A Sex Crazed Culture

By now, everybody is aware of teen icon Miley Cyrus's performance at MTV's Video Music Awards show on August 25th. Apparently, "Hannah Montana" wanted to send a message that she is all grown up now, and she did just that. It was certainly a calculated move by the twenty-year-old pop star, taking a page out of Madonna's playbook, and it seems to have worked. She accomplished what she set out to accomplish. Her performance has now been shown over and over again on just about every single news station. Even those who are mortified over what happened seem to enjoy watching the clip repeatedly. Now, all the rap artists want Miley in their music videos, and why wouldn't they? Meanwhile, the US weighs its options as to whether to respond to the Syrian regime's decision to use chemical weapons against its own people, a very difficult predicament. Surprisingly, Miley remained the number one news story for quite a while. Why is that?

Sex sells in our culture. We are a culture absolutely obsessed with sexuality and sexual expression, and as the digital age progresses, this becomes more and more the case. Some will say, who can blame us? God has given us a sex drive, and there is nothing we can do about it. Marilyn Monroe once said, "Sex is a part of nature, and I go along with nature." But for parents, this overtly sexual expression that is constantly in our faces makes raising children and instilling values into them incredibly challenging and difficult, yet more necessary than ever. It serves us well to take a minute and ponder what the real issues are here that lie under the surface of our culture's sex obsession—intimacy, self-confidence, body image, power, control, loneliness, affirmation, and acceptance. These are the deep issues at hand that so often go unspoken. These are the issues that need to be addressed, talked about, and dealt with.

There is another story that has dominated the news here in Nashville in recent weeks, and that is the situation with four Vanderbilt football players. Just like in the Penn State scandal, I don't believe you can judge an entire team or community based on the reckless and irresponsible actions of a few individuals. Vanderbilt remains a great school, and this situation is incredibly unfortunate on many levels. The judicial process will run its course. However, I cannot help but wonder about the link between our culture's sex obsession and these types of instances. What can we do to teach our kids that sex is not something to be exploited, forced, bought, or sold? Sex is the way that two consenting adults express their love for each other in an intimate setting. I used to travel and speak on college campuses, and I would tell the students that if they decided to go to bed with somebody, they should be open to the possibility of spending the rest of their lives with that person. They should be aware of the realistic possibility that a child might be conceived. You should have seen some of the looks I got. Still, many don't want to take responsibility for their actions. John Barrymore once said that, "Sex is the thing that takes up the least amount of time but causes the most amount of trouble." Our culture continues to move away from viewing sex as an expression of intimacy and love to one where sex is glorified and objectified, used and abused. As a result, sex loses its luster in marriages and committed relationships. This may very well be contributing to our high divorce rates and rising restlessness in marriage.

We simply don't understand what sex is and when it is appropriate. It is imperative that parents talk to their kids at some point about sex, what it is, and what it isn't. And my advice is, don't wait too long to have that conversation. The age will be different for every child and family. Sure, it's an awkward conversation to have, but if you don't have it, the culture will.

37. The Challenge of Personal Growth

Historically, Lent is viewed as a time of penitence, self-reflection, and personal growth leading up to Easter, reminiscent of the time Jesus spent alone in the wilderness. However, in this day and age, many are simply not up for the challenge. Why? Personal growth is difficult and coming to terms with our shortcomings and character flaws is always uncomfortable. The nine personality types of the Enneagram can be a helpful tool. Jesus asks a timeless question in the Sermon on the Mount: "Why do you see the speck in your neighbor's eye but fail to recognize the log in your own eye?" Jordan Peterson, a well-known Canadian Psychologist who taught at Harvard and now at the University of Toronto, recently published a fascinating new book: *12 Rules for Life: An Antidote to Chaos* (Random House). His fourth rule is this: "Compare yourself to who you were yesterday, not to who somebody else is today."

This sounds simple, but it's not. We live in a culture of competition and ongoing comparison. Social media has taken this to new levels, constantly reminding us of what other people have that we do not. When we become preoccupied with everybody else's life, we often think of our own as being inadequate. They got a new house. They got a new car. They went on an expensive vacation. Why can't we do that? Peterson advises, "Consult your resentment. It's a revelatory emotion, for all its pathology. It's part of an evil triad: arrogance, deceit, and resentment. Nothing causes more harm than this underworld Trinity." Of course, resentment comes in many form, but it becomes toxic very quickly. Everybody's life is different. We all see the world through our own lens and experience. Is there inequality, injustice, and a lack of opportunity for many? Yes. That seems obvious. It provides a never-ending opportunity to serve others and to show compassion. But when we become too obsessed with the lives of others, whether they have more or less, it blinds us to our own shortcomings and blessings.

Peterson's sixth rule is also relevant: "Set your house in perfect order before you criticize the world." The trend in our culture is to do the exact opposite: focus on what's wrong with everybody else to keep us distracted from the difficult task of personal growth and responsibility. It also holds true that we point out in other people the very things we dislike about ourselves. That person is materialistic. That person is selfish. That person is irritable. That person is a liar. Peterson reminds us that we all have serious inner work to do. He says, "Start small. Are you working hard on your career, or even your job, or are you letting bitterness and resentment hold you back and drag you down? Have you made peace with your brother? Are you treating your spouse and your children with dignity and respect? Do you have habits that are destroying your health and well-being? Have you said what you need to say to your friends and family members?" The difficult work of self-reflection and personal growth is often ignored in a culture that shuns responsibility, criticizes quickly, and blames others for everything. It is a disturbing trend that needs to change, and that change can start with a long look into our own hearts.

III

THE CHRISTIAN LIFE

38. The Many "Brands" of Christianity

Socrates famously said, "The unexamined life is not worth living." One of my favorite questions to ask is: "Why are you a Christian?" As you might imagine, the responses are usually all over the place. "I'm a Christian because I was born into a Christian family. I'm a Christian because that's what good people do. I'm a Christian because Jesus died for my sins. I'm a Christian because I care about other people. I'm a Christian because I want to go to heaven one day when I die." None of these answers are necessarily wrong. We should all wrestle with this important question in a culture where many people are Christians just because they feel that's what's expected. Biblical Scholar Marcus Borg recently published a book called *Convictions*, and in the first chapter of that book, he talks about 5 basic categories of Christians in American culture:

CONSERVATIVE CHRISTIANS—believe that the Bible is the literal, infallible, inerrant Word of God. Conservative Christians believe that how we live here and now will determine where we spend eternity, that Jesus died to pay for our sins, and that the only way to heaven is to believe in Jesus Christ. Conservative Christians are often very interested in moral issues like abortion, issues of sexuality, and living the moral life. Often things like drinking, smoking, and gambling are concerns of many conservative Christians.

CONVENTIONAL CHRISTIANS—represent the Christian middle today. Conventional Christians have often been Christians their entire lives. They are not as committed to biblical inerrancy and doctrinal orthodoxy as Conservative Christians. But they are certainly very familiar with church language and traditions.

UNCERTAIN CHRISTIANS—These folks are unsure what to make of certain conventional and conservative Christian teachings. They ask questions like: Is the Bible the literal word of God and is it inerrant? Was Jesus really born of a virgin? Did he really perform all the miracles we find in the gospels? Did Jesus have to die for our sins? Is Christianity the only way to salvation? But despite asking these questions and sometimes not knowing the answers, uncertain Christians continue to be a part of the church.

FORMER CHRISTIANS—These are people who have left the church for whatever reason. This group often considers themselves spiritual but not religious. And for many of them, they have left because the version of Christianity that they learned growing up is no longer convincing. But many still hang on to the periphery of the church especially around high holy days like Christmas and Easter.

PROGRESSIVE CHRISTIANS—Generally speaking, Progressive Christians reject the concept of biblical inerrancy and literal interpretation but still believe that the Bible speaks God's truth. Salvation is primarily about transformation in this world and not just life after death. Jesus is the decisive revelation of God, God in human form. Believing is not as important as transformation. And many progressive Christians are found in mainline denominations. (Marcus Borg, *Convictions*)

Which category describes your faith? It may be difficult to pick just one. Just as there are all different kinds of churches in a town like Nashville, there are also all different kinds of Christians. I've come to believe that perhaps we place too much emphasis on the type of Christian that we are rather than focusing on whether we take our faith seriously or just culturally. At the end of the day, the category you choose is not nearly as important as whether your faith transforms your life, words, and actions.

39. The Core of Christianity

Dr. Rubel Shelly served as the long-term minister of Woodmont Hills Church of Christ here in Nashville for about twenty-seven years before going on to serve as the president of Rochester College up in Michigan. He has a book titled *I Knew Jesus before he was a Christian…and I Liked Him Better Then*. His basic claim is that the Jesus of history and the Jesus of common public perception are two very different persons. He feels that the church has done a poor job of representing Jesus and his message over the past two thousand years to the extent that he has become unattractive to many, many people today. He quotes American scholar Sam Pascoe in saying that, "Christianity was born in Israel, only to be taken to Greece and morphed into a philosophy. From there it was taken to Rome and made into an institution of civil power. Eventually it migrated into Europe where it was developed into a culture. And later, it was brought to America and made into an entrepreneurial business enterprise." These are strong words, but they ring true in many ways.

Rubel Shelly says that when we institutionalized Jesus, we watered down core parts of his message and we started to become more concerned with maintenance, doctrine, correct beliefs, power, and blending Jesus with the culture. And so now what we have in our culture is a lot of people who really don't know what Jesus was all about because the church has misrepresented him for so long. We've made him into what we want him to be rather than allow his message to speak for itself. We have tried to put Jesus in a box. In some ways, we have tried to put words into his mouth.

Mark tells us in chapter 12 that a scribe comes along and asks Jesus, "Which commandment is the first of all?" And Jesus responds with: "Hear O Israel: The Lord our God, the Lord is One;" and then he says, "You shall love the Lord your God with all your heart, and with all your soul, and with all your mind, and with all your strength. And the second commandment is like it: you shall love your neighbor as yourself. There is no other commandment greater than these." That's it! That's what the Christian life is all about. It is very straightforward. Yet if we are honest, we know that we have a hard time following these two commandments. They are simple, and we know them by heart, yet they are very difficult and complex at the same time.

Methodist pastor Martin Thielen has said this: "Of all the things that clamor for our time, energy, and attention, what matters most? What is the bottom line? It's a crucial question. We are all constantly bombarded with dozens of concerns, including our job, career, marriage, children, home, friends, faith, church, community, health, and finances. And these concerns often compete with one another for our time and energy. So how do we figure out what matters most? What is primary? What is secondary? What really counts? That's what this scribe in Mark 12 is trying to figure out. He wanted to know, what is the greatest priority in life?"

Jesus answers him by saying that our lives should be focused on having a relationship with God and a relationship with others, and it should happen in that order. Before we get too wrapped up with doctrine, biblical literalism, worship styles, social issues, and church shopping, we should ask ourselves, "How are we doing when it comes to following these two commandments?" That will tell us a lot about our life and our faith. I grew up as a preacher's kids hearing my father talk about the cross. The vertical bar represents our relationship to God (worship, prayer, Bible Study, etc.) and the horizontal bar represents our relationship to others (mission, service, outreach, kindness). Without both bars, we don't have the cross. Without both aspects of the faith, we don't have a complete faith.

40. Christianity in an Age of Trump

In my doctoral work at Sewanee, I focused primarily on the intersection of faith and politics and the great challenge it presents for preachers and churches in the twenty-first century. For years I have been concerned about the growing polarization and lack of civility in our culture that has taken its toll on churches, denominations, families, and friendships. I have also been very critical of what I will call "close minded liberalism" that attempts to silence any voice that is not progressive. What has happened on many college campuses is truly sad. Jonathan Haidt calls it the "Coddling of the American Mind." The election of Donald Trump to the presidency was the culmination of multiple factors coming together at one time including a belief that the country had moved too far to the left; political elites in both parties neglecting the working class in America; stagnant wages; loss of jobs; the rise of ISIS; fear of illegal immigration and a nation quickly becoming more diverse. Add this to the simple reality that there are multiple worldviews of what America is and should become.

Perhaps the most perplexing part of Trump's rise to power has been the blind embrace and endorsement by many evangelical Christians who are very quick to overlook and dismiss issues of character and morality that should matter to Christians. Many will say, "Well, we elected a president and not a preacher. He's getting the job done." Trump is a master entertainer. He has successfully integrated reality TV into government and although the media will never admit it, he helps their ratings. History will prove whether he is an effective president and what his political accomplishments are. Denuclearization of the Korean Peninsula would be an incredible achievement for any president and a significant step towards world peace. However, as our culture continues its rapid pace of secularization, what seems to be missing are some of the core values, grounded by faith traditions, which made this nation great to begin with. This includes treating each other with civility and respect; telling the truth; loving our neighbor as ourselves; welcoming the tired, lonely, and downtrodden; being faithful to our spouses; embracing a sense of humility; taking the log out of our own eye; being reminded that we do not worship money and wealth but God alone; and recognizing that all people are created equal and deserve to be treated with respect.

My seven-year-old daughter walked into the room when Stormy Daniels was being interviewed and asked me who she was. That's a tough one to answer. I would argue that political loyalty should never be an excuse for overlooking moral accountability. When it comes to the American presidency, character and values matter just as much as politics. As a centrist and a moderate, I believe in the concept of Aristotle's Golden Mean, the healthy point between two extremes. Nobody has a monopoly on the truth. The President is human with shortcomings and flaws. We should never become self-righteous and pretend that we have it all figured out, but foundational values and moral leadership have always mattered in that office, and whether we have a Republican or Democratic occupying the White House, nobody gets a pass simply on the basis of partisanship.

41. Dangerous Versus Healthy Religion

As we reflect upon what happened in Oslo, Norway a few weeks ago and as we prepare for the ten-year anniversary of September 11. 2001, we should be reminded that religion remains the most powerful source for both good and evil in our day. I am convinced that many who consider themselves nonreligious or secular are not responding to religion in general but to a particular kind of dangerous religion. What do I mean? Here's the difference:

DANGEROUS RELIGION says that God wants you to kill innocent people to make a statement. HEALTHY RELIGION says that God is the creator of all life and would never want us to kill innocent people under any circumstance.

DANGEROUS RELIGION says that if you don't see things my way, then I don't want anything to do with you. HEALTHY RELIGION says you may not agree with me, but I can respect the opinion that you have, and I want you to respect mine.

DANGEROUS RELIGION says that God is on the side of only one nation and wants it to become an empire. HEALTHY RELIGION says that people of all nations are children of God and should work together to live in peace.

DANGEROUS RELIGION says you have to be of a certain race or socio-economic class to be a part of the church. HEALTHY RELIGION says that we must learn to live together in a diverse world with people of different worldviews, opinions, and faith backgrounds.

DANGEROUS RELIGION says that if you have messed up or made a mistake in life, then you will always have that mark on your record. HEALTHY RELIGION says that if you've messed up and made a mistake in life, you've probably already suffered the consequences; but God forgives you, gives you a clean slate, and wants you to keep moving forward in life.

DANGEROUS RELIGION says there cannot be a just and loving God because of all the pain and suffering in this world. HEALTHY RELIGION says that we have free will and God does not control everything. When we suffer in life, God suffers with us.

DANGEROUS RELIGION says if you pray hard enough for wealth and prosperity, it will be yours for the taking. HEALTHY RELIGION says God does not define wealth and prosperity by the same standards of this world.

DANGEROUS RELIGION says if you don't interpret that passage of scripture the same way I do, then you are wrong. HEALTHY RELIGION says there may be multiple interpretations of that passage and what speaks to me may be very different than what speaks to you...but that's OK.

DANGEROUS RELIGION says, "what can the church do to serve the needs of me and my needs?" HEALTHY RELIGION says, "what can I do to serve the church and to meet the needs of our community?"

DANGEROUS RELIGION says I want nothing to do with you because you have hurt me in the past. HEALTHY religion says turn the other cheek, go the extra mile, give them your cloak as well, forgive seventy times seven.

42. The Best of Liberal and Conservative Christianity

In many ways, Christianity remains as polarized as the larger culture. Of course, there is great irony in this fact given Jesus' prayer that "all would be one so the world might believe." Jesus knew that division among believers would prove problematic, and it has. The strength of conservative Christianity has been its emphasis on personal transformation— being saved or born again. Its weakness has been its neglect of the Kingdom of God. The strength of liberal Christianity has been its emphasis on bringing the kingdom of God to earth—mission, social justice, outreach, inclusion. But it often neglects the importance of personal transformation. To understand the "Kingdom of God" the way Jesus talked about it means that we must find the balance between spiritual (personal) and political (social) transformation. The message of Jesus is about both. The Kingdom of God is what the world would look like if God were in charge and the rulers of this world weren't. The truth is, we need both, not just one or the other. This world is far from perfect, with many problems, and Jesus is constantly challenging us to bring the kingdom of God to earth as it is in heaven. George Buttrick once said, "If religion doesn't begin with the individual, it doesn't begin. But if it ends with the individual, it ends." I grew up hearing my father talk about the cross. The vertical bar of the cross represents our relationship with God: worship, prayer, Bible study. The horizontal bar represents our relationships with others: mission, service, relationships. Without both bars, you don't have a cross. Without both aspects of the faith, Christianity is incomplete.

43. When Tolerance Becomes Intolerant

A few weeks ago, Dr. James Hudnut Beumler, professor of American religious history and former Dean of Vanderbilt Divinity School, came to our church to give a presentation on "the future of the mainline church," a topic he has now been researching for years. I was intrigued to hear his remarks and analysis. We are all aware that the mainline church (Presbyterian, Methodist, Episcopal, Lutheran, etc.) has been in steady decline for decades in this country. The drop in membership numbers are staggering and quite frankly, depressing. Dr. Hudnut Beumler alluded to many reasons for this decline: aging membership, denominational devaluation, secularization, and a failure to reach millennials. However, there is one reason he did not mention that I have gradually come to believe to be true: the lauded "tolerance" of the mainline church has, in many ways, now become intolerant.

What does that mean? Conservatives and moderates have been ostracized and marginalized from many mainline congregations. Perhaps it was the religious right and the moral majority who set the stage for this in the 1980's, but the mainline church responded by moving way too far to the left, and the result has not been good. To be clear, I am not advocating that the mainline church embrace literalism, fundamentalism, theocracy, or fear-based theology. That will not happen, nor should it. What I am advocating is that the mainline church should learn to make room at the table for more conservative and moderate Christians who, for example, may find themselves pro-life, supporters of traditional marriage, or a member of the Republican Party. In many mainline congregations, these folks no longer feel welcomed, but judged.

The liberalization of the mainline church since the mid-twentieth century, however well-intentioned, has now set us up for a future that is bleak at best. In the Presbyterian Church (USA), larger congregations which tend to be more conservative are gradually leaving the denomination. Or, as I have heard many pastors say, "the denomination left us." Meanwhile, more evangelical churches that are not obsessed with social issues are growing and reaching new people. These are the churches that do not spend all of their time and energy fighting over controversial topics that only divide and distract. In his book *The Intolerance of Tolerance*, Don Carson says, "The notion of tolerance is changing…and the sad reality is that this new, contemporary tolerance is intrinsically intolerant. It is blind to its own shortcomings because it erroneously thinks it holds the moral high ground; it cannot be questioned because it has become part of the West's plausibility structure. Worse, this new tolerance is socially dangerous and is certainly intellectually debilitating. Even the good that it wishes to achieve is better accomplished in other ways." Phillip Yancy echoes this sentiment in his book *What's So Amazing About Grace*, when he says, "Nowadays legalism has changed its focus. In a thoroughly secular culture, the church is more likely to show un-grace through a spirit of moral superiority or a fierce attitude toward opponents in the culture wars." That can cut both ways. The church of the future would do well to guard against Christian tribalism, recognize that multiple ideologies exist, and learn to graciously make room at the table for all perspectives. Only time will tell if we can do that.

44. What Does It Mean to Live in Faith?

Many misunderstandings exist in our culture as to what it means to live a life of faith. At its very core, this question lies at the heart of all theology, a field that will never be exhausted or mastered. Having faith in God does not mean that everything in life will work out just the way we plan. It does not mean that we will be spared hardship and pain, tragedy and suffering. Faith in God does not mean simply biding our time and waiting to go to heaven one day when we die. It does not mean that there is a master puppeteer in the sky, orchestrating our every move. Humans do have free will. Bad things do happen to us all. Pain and suffering are real, so then what is faith, and what does it mean to be a person of faith?

The writer to the Hebrews gives this definition: "Faith is the assurance of things hoped for, the conviction of things not seen." According to these words, faith and hope are intertwined, two sides of the same coin, perhaps inseparable. St. Augustine once said that, "Faith is to believe what you do not see; the reward of this faith is to see what you believe." Thomas Aquinas once said, "To one who has faith, no explanation is necessary; to one without faith, no explanation is possible." Charles Spurgeon preached that, "Faith obliterates time, annihilates distance, and brings future things at once into its possession." Emmanuel Teney once argued that, "As our faith is strengthened, we will find that there is no longer a need to have a sense of control; things will flow as they will and to our great delight and benefit, we will flow with them." The truth is, there is no one definitive definition of faith. Faith is a way of being, a way of living, a way of approaching the future. It involves being always open to the spirit. Faith is what gives us courage in the face of fear and hope in the face of disappointment. Faith is trusting that life will go on, even after bad things happen. Faith means learning to not be trapped or owned by things that have happened in the past. The past should not and does not define us. Guilt and shame can be overcome. Faith is learning to see the world through a different lens. It's not an escape from reality but a refusal to accept that this is all that there is. There is always more.

Faith means believing that we can leave the world better than we found it. Faith involves not getting bogged down by the trivial matters of life, the things that really don't matter in the big picture. Living in faith means moving beyond a world of superficiality, materialism, resentment, and control. It is embracing the mystery of creation and the joy of every day existence. Living in faith means reminding ourselves that we are all on a journey. and we simply don't know or control the future. Therefore humility, gratitude, love, and presence matter every step of the way.

45. A Season of Soul Searching

Lent is the forty-day period leading up to Easter, reminiscent of the time Jesus spent alone in the wilderness before beginning his public ministry. It is a season of soul-searching and spiritual growth. If we are honest, we might all admit we are very good at identifying what is wrong with other people. We are good at naming the character flaws and shortcomings of others and the way others live their lives. Criticizing others is neither difficult nor original. It is an easy way to keep the focus off ourselves. Jesus offers us a better question in the Sermon on the Mount: "Why do you see the speck in your neighbor's eye but fail to recognize the log in your own eye. First, remove the log from your own eye and then you can see clearly the speck in your neighbor's eye." The problem? Sometimes it' hard to come to terms with the log in our own eye. It takes humility, courage, and a dose of reality. Sometimes we need help naming our own shortcomings. But we should stop and ask: What do I need to work on? Where do I fall short? How can I become a better person?

Lent is a good time to take a long look in the mirror, not to beat ourselves up over where we fall short but to identify one or two things that we need to work on between now and Easter and then work on it. Perhaps it's anger and a temper; maybe it's worry and fear; maybe it's stress; maybe its eating too much or drinking too much; maybe it's our marriage or family situation; maybe it's spending more quality time with our children and actually being present; maybe it's being too judgmental and intolerant; maybe it's being overly addicted to social media, spending too much time on our phones; maybe we need to set aside quiet time for prayer and reflection. In his book *Emotionally Healthy Spirituality*, New York City pastor Peter Scazzero identifies ten specific symptoms of Emotionally Unhealthy Spirituality. These include: Using God to run from God (religious busyness); Ignoring the emotions of anger, sadness, and fear; Dying to the wrong things (living a miserable life); denying the past's impact on the present; Dividing our lives into "secular" and "sacred"; Doing for God instead of being with God; Spiritualizing away conflict; Covering over brokenness, weakness, and failure; Living without limits or boundaries; Judging other people's spiritual journey. Scazzaro argues that these things must be replaced with "emotionally healthy spirituality" which involves slowing down, anchoring in God's love, and freeing ourselves from false illusions that do not necessarily align with reality. Lent is certainly the season to improve our own spiritual lives and we will all do that very differently. There is a strong correlation between spiritual vitality and emotional well-being. We cannot have one without the other. Lent gives us a chance to work on both.

46. Between Good Friday and Easter

I recently had a conversation with a prominent therapist in town who told me that most of the clients he sees come into his office at 5 pm on the Saturday before Easter. He did not mean that literally, but metaphorically and symbolically. Life is full of Saturdays. The worst has happened. Plans have changed. What we thought would be true seems no longer true. The marriage is over. The affair has been discovered. The suicide took place. The cancer is real. The child is in rehab. The job has been lost. Bankruptcy has been filed. The addiction continues. The fetus has lost its heartbeat. Yes, life does not seem to work out the way we originally planned which can leave many of us hopeless, lost, confused, angry, resentful, and overwhelmed.

Freud once said that pain comes to us in life from three different forms: first, from the natural world with its hurricanes, tornadoes, floods, and earthquakes; second, from our bodies which decline over time as we age; and third, the most difficult, from the pain that we inflict upon each other. It's the disappointment that happens when those we love the most hurt us and hurt us deeply. The disciples were in despair following the crucifixion. The one they had loved, trusted, followed, and believed in had been executed, put to death in the most violent of ways. It seemed like it was over. The movement that had given them great hope and meaning had ended. Jesus was dead. But thankfully, the story doesn't end there. Death and despair never have the final word when it comes to God. In Luke's Gospel, when the women went to the tomb early on the third day, they found that the stone had been rolled away, and they went inside and did not find the body. Two men appeared in dazzling white clothes and tried to console the grieving women. They asked them a profound question, "Why do you look for the living among the dead? He is not here. He is risen."

There are many messages of Easter, and churches will be filled all over the world to hear them. At the heart of Easter is a reminder that death is not the end. There is eternal life. God can take any type of hopelessness, despair, and pain in this life and turn it into a new beginning. There are many Good Friday Christians in our world who live with their heads down, their hopes dashed, their expectations lowered, and their fears out of control. There are many who live as though they would rather not be here, as though life is a burden and not a blessing, and although they are alive in this world, they are simply going through the motions day after day. But Easter can keep us from looking at life this way. Easter reminds us to live in hope and not despair. Author Frederick Buechner was once asked if he had been born again. He gave a classic response: "Let me tell you something, I have been born again and again and again." No matter what may happen to us in life, may we live in hope and always be born again, and again, and again.

47. Easter Christians

I am convinced that not all Christians are truly Easter Christians. Not all of them live a life as though they believe in the risen Christ. Nothing excites them, nothing inspires them, and everything is an inconvenience. Their cantankerous spirits are contagious, their pessimism is annoying, their complaining is relentless, and they pull other people down.

But Easter Christians don't look at life this way. Easter Christians are different. Easter Christians are truly alive. Bad things happen to all of us. Illness, divorce, infertility, loss of a family member, loss of a job, addictions, depression, anxiety, betrayal—the list could go on an on. Many of these things we can control and many of them we can't. But what we can control is the way that we respond to the setbacks of life. Perhaps Paul says it best in II Corinthians when he states, "This extraordinary power belongs to God and does not come from us. We are afflicted in every way, but not crushed; perplexed, but not driven to despair; persecuted, but not forsaken; struck down, but not destroyed."

Easter reminds us that there is absolutely nothing in this world that cannot be overcome as long as we have faith and a firm belief that because of Christ, God is there to suffer with us and God calls us to never give up and to never quit in the midst of our greatest struggles. A friend and colleague of mine, Scott Colglazier, puts it this way: "There is resurrection all around us. Every day there is resurrection. Daily there are moments when life breaks through. Maybe we can't explain it or predict it or schedule it, but if we have eyes to see and hearts to feel, it is there. Awe. Wonder. Joy. It's in the eyes of someone you love. It's in the human stories of love triumphing over hate. It's in the presence of God enduring with us when we go through some of our little moments of dying" (*Finding A Faith That Makes Sense*). When we go through hard times, and all of us do, we have to keep moving forward knowing that it's up to us to bounce back and with God's help we can.

Are you an Easter Christian? Do you believe in the risen Christ? I hope that you do!

48. Five Lessons from Billy Graham

Billy Graham passed away peacefully on February 21, 2018 at his family home in Montreat, NC. Many have referred to him as the most influential preacher since the Apostle Paul. That would be difficult to argue. An advisor to twelve different US Presidents, Graham traveled the world preaching the gospel of Jesus Christ in stadiums and arenas on multiple continents. There are many lessons for both the mainline and evangelical church to learn from the life of Billy Graham.

First, he was committed to the Bible. He believed that the Bible speaks God's truth throughout the ages. Graham did not dismiss scholarship, but he believed with all his heart in the transforming power of God's word. He preached it boldly and without apology. Graham had the utmost confidence that the word of God speaks for itself, and his sermons were full of scripture. A common theme in his message was repentance and second chances.

Second, Graham demonstrated the relevance of the gospel to political life without becoming overtly partisan. Somebody once tried to corner Graham on a contentious political issue to see where he really stood. Graham responded: "I look at the birds of the sky. They have a right wing and a left wing, and it takes both to fly." Graham counseled both Republican and Democratic presidents without getting bogged down in the partisan fray. He knew that the gospel message transcended partisan politics. The Mainline church has often become far too obsessed with politics and contentious social issues that simply divide the body of Christ.

Third, Billy Graham stood firm in the face of criticism. He was attacked and denounced by fundamentalists and liberals alike. Graham would reach out to his detractors both publicly and privately and work to reconcile. He turned the other cheek and did not respond harshly. Yet, Graham was fully aware that part of being a leader and a public figure was learning to face criticism, and he did so with courage and grace. He recognized that if you dabble in politics, you can expect to be betrayed. After all, Nixon secretly recorded their personal conversations.

Fourth, Graham lived a life of character and integrity. He was the same person in private that he was in public. He had nothing to hide. He was always honest about missteps and regrets, one of them being how often he was away from his family because of his calling and schedule. He was faithful and committed to his wife Ruth for sixty-four years. He and Ruth loved their children, and they passed their faith along to them.

Lastly, Graham knew that, for Christians, there was no substitute for an authentic, personal relationship with Christ. In an age of cultural Christianity, this is very important. He was once invited to preach at Duke Chapel the first year Will Willimon was the minister there. After the service, standing in Willimon's office, Graham said: "You will have a great ministry here and I wish you well. But many of these folks are simply unaware that Christ is eager to have them." Graham knew that discipleship involves commitment, passion, and sacrifice. It is not convenient or comfortable.

49. On Practicing What We Preach

A few years ago, there was a survey that was conducted by Thom Ranier, President of Lifeway Christian Resources based right here in Nashville. For over a decade, Ranier has been researching the "unchurched" people of our society to find out why they are hesitant to get involved in the church. And the results of this survey were very interesting. Contrary to popular belief, Ranier says that non-Christians are not turned off by the church, by preaching, by Sunday School, or even by evangelism. But there were some other things that bothered them about the Christian community. These included:

1. Christians who treat other Christians poorly. "The unchurched don't expect Christians to be perfect, but they can't understand why we treat each other without dignity and respect."

2. Non-Christians are bothered by "holier-than-thou" attitudes. "The unchurched know that Christians will make mistakes, and they often have a forgiving attitude when we mess up. But they are repulsed when Christians act superior to them."

3. Non-Christians are bothered by Christians who talk more than they listen. "Many of the unchurched, at some point, have a perception that a Christian is a person who can offer a sympathetic and listening ear. Unfortunately, many of the unchurched thought that Christians were too busy talking to listen to them.

4. Lastly, Ranier reports that non-Christians are bothered by Christians who don't go to church or very rarely attend church. "They saw the disconnect between belief and prac-

tice in the lives of Christians who never or very rarely attended church."

Ranier concludes his research by saying, "They are all aware that any human will stumble at times, but these unchurched individuals want to know that Christians will treat each other well and they want to see humility in our lives. They want to know that we will take the time to listen, and even take more time to really be involved in their lives. And they want to know that we love our churches and that we are committed to supporting them."

When you read the gospels, it's clear that Jesus really didn't think a whole lot of religious talk. He said "beware of wolves in sheep's clothing. You will know them by their fruit." He denounced the scribes and Pharisees who could quote scripture, use fancy words, say fancy prayers, and make theological statements to impress people. Jesus was much more interested in faith that led to action—especially actions of love, kindness, and compassion. I have found that nothing is more dangerous or scary than a manipulative person hiding under a Christian disguise. The common disconnect between what we say we believe and what we do is the greatest challenge for Christians. Words simply don't matter if they are not backed up by actions. People pay more attention to what you do than to what you say. Harvey Cox says we've officially moved from the age of belief to the age of the spirit, and I agree. You know what I think will continue to mark this new era of Christianity—a complete intolerance for those who cannot practice or at least authentically try to practice what they say they believe in. In the age of the spirit, talk is cheap. Actions will speak louder than words.

50. Christian Hypocrisy and the Kingdom of God

In conversations that I have had over the years with those who are not Christian or who might call themselves disengaged or disillusioned Christians, the subject of hypocrisy often arises. How can Christians say they believe what Jesus taught if they fail to live it? To be more specific, how can you read the Sermon on the Mount but still support war and violence? How can you claim to believe in forgiveness but hold onto grudges and resentments forever? How can you love your neighbor but judge those who are different? How can you care for the poor but never do anything to help them? How can you say the church is important but then never show up or support it? These are all fair and valid questions. These are questions that people of faith must take on and discuss? Christian hypocrisy does exist, and it's not new. However, what matters is not if we fall short, but whether or not we are always trying to do better. Jesus came to proclaim the Kingdom of God, a way of living that is not easy or convenient. In this Kingdom, the last will be first, the peacemakers are blessed, and the other cheek is turned. In this kingdom, we are called to forgive over and over, love enemies, not worship money, pray regularly, stop worrying, and treat others the way we want to be treated. That's a high bar. The kingdom of God is an ideal that Christians should strive to bring to earth. It's anything but easy.

In his book on the Sermon on the Mount, Franciscan priest Richard Rohr says, "The temptation of all Churches is to think they are a gathering of the saved, the born-again elite ones, on the right side of the eternal border." Churches should be places where everybody is welcome because nobody is perfect. Does that mean that standards don't exist? Of course not. But the ideals are so high that we all fall short in our own way. To some degree, we are all hypocrites, but we keep trying again and again. Rohr says that if you meet a Kingdom person, you'll know it: "They are surrendered people. You sense that life is OK at their core. They have given control to Another and are at peace.

A Kingdom person lives for what matters, for life in its deepest sense. There is a kind of gentle absolutism about their lifestyle, a kind of calm freedom." Kingdom people recognize their spiritual shortcomings, are humble, hunger for righteousness, show mercy, and are pure in heart. When it comes to the Kingdom of God, motive always matters and so does telling the truth. Kingdom people are always striving to do better. Perhaps most importantly, Kingdom people have come to terms with issues of power and control. Control freaks will always struggle in seeking the kingdom of God. Must we simply become complacent, passive, and victims to life's circumstances? Not necessarily. But as long as we are trying to control everything, inner peace will be a challenge. Jesus offers a healthy prescription for a world based on money and power, greed and selfishness, fear and control, materialism and superficiality. Some will decide to seek it, others will not. We all fall short in the search, but the journey is worth it.

51. Partisan Divisions within Churches

We live in a nation with a unique religious history. Nashvillian Jon Meacham makes this case very well in his 2006 book *American Gospel: God, the Founding Fathers, and the Making of a Nation.* He writes, "The great goodness about America—the American Gospel, if you will—is that religion shapes the life of the nation without strangling it. Belief in God is central to the country's experience, yet for the broad center, faith is a matter of choice, not coercion, and the legacy of the Founding Fathers is that the sensible center holds." Meacham clearly indicates that the Founding Fathers sought to establish a nation where religious freedom was pivotal and could not be taken away by the government or any human being. The *Declaration of Independence* states that, "All men are created equal and are endowed by their Creator with inherent and inalienable rights." Thomas Jefferson and the other founders struggled to find the proper place for religion in American life. In hindsight, their endeavor proved successful. The Founders' intention was to create a Republic that maintained a separation of church and state, but in no way did that mean a complete separation of faith and politics. However, it gets very interesting when partisan politics enter congregations and the pulpit.

In 2012, Mike Slaughter, Charles Gutenson, and Robert Jones published a book entitled *Hijacked: Responding to the Partisan Church Divide.* The authors frame the question well. They ask, "Why is it, then, that we have allowed political partisanship to enter so deeply into our churches? And, perhaps more importantly, how is it that we have allowed those differences to divide us, to create obstacles among us, and to have created an environment in which one or the other can be somehow considered less a 'follower of Jesus' simply on the basis of one being the supporter of a particular party or ideology." They argue that many people in our society believe that if you are a Christian, you will identify with a particular party and hold deep convictions on certain issues. Everything is black and white. If that is true, then who is right: Jerry Falwell or Al Sharpton? Pat Robertson or Jim Wallis? Slaughter and Gutenson believe that it becomes problematic when Christians combine theology with a certain brand of politics and try to categorize everybody in one of two camps. They argue, "It seems popular lore in contemporary American culture to assume that there are only two theopolitical positions. According to the popular way of categorizing people, there are conservatives and liberals. If you are conservative, then you are politically and theologically conservative; if you are liberal, then you are politically and theologically liberal." These words, "liberal" and "conservative," are loaded words in our culture. Everybody has a different understanding of what they mean. "One can be theologically conservative and politically conservative; one can be theologically liberal and politically conservative; one can be theologically conservative and theologically liberal; and one can be theologically liberal and politically liberal." Simply throwing around these terms proves unhelpful. No one political party has a monopoly on Christianity. Churches and pastors must accept this fact and advocate for a respectful dialogue that is grounded in Christian love. Our culture seems to have a low tolerance for disagreement and alternative perspectives. If the church can't set an example, then how will it ever happen in the culture at large?

52. Could the Church Save the World?

Karl Barth served as a mentor and friend to Dietrich Bonhoeffer. In 1933, while Bonhoeffer was on a ministerial sojourn to England, Barth sent him a terse and poignant letter from his homeland: "You are a German...the house of your church is on fire...you must return to your post by the next ship." Bonhoeffer needed to return home immediately. If the great Swiss theologian were alive today, I wonder what he would say about twenty-first century America. There is clearly a force that threatens to tear this nation apart and that is the force of political and ideological polarization. We now live in one of the most divisive times that this country has ever seen, and it's been building for some time. Differing ideologies are present even within the same political party.

If these divides have always been present, social media has managed to take it to new levels. In a September article for New York Magazine, Andrew Sullivan writes these words about the danger that excessive tribalism poses to our democracy: "Two tribes whose mutual incomprehension and loathing can drown out their love of country, each of whom scans current events almost entirely to see if they advance not so much their country's interests but their own. I mean two tribes where one contains most racial minorities and the other is disproportionately white; where one tribe lives on the coasts and in the cities and the other is scattered across a rural and exurban expanse; where one tribe holds on to traditional faith and the other is increasingly contemptuous of religion altogether; where one is viscerally nationalist and the other's outlook is increasingly global; where each dominates a major political party; and, most dangerously, where both are growing in intensity as they move further apart." Some of these claims might be considered broad generalizations. Whether or not you agree with Sullivan, it is hard to argue that extreme tribalism is real and is causing many problems.

Throughout history, Christianity has been guilty of playing a role in deepening this divide. American Christianity is often broken down into liberal and conservative, fundamentalist and modernist, mainline and evangelical. But now, it's time for the church to step up, do its job, bring people together, accept basic differences as a part of life, and honor Jesus' prayer in John 17 that "all would be one so the world might believe." It's time for the church to become a place where people of different ideologies, politics, denominations, and backgrounds can come together out of love and respect for each other. The church should be a place where important issues are analyzed and discussed through the lens of the gospel. Complex issues like health care, immigration, poverty, racism, guns, and just war should be talked about and not ignored. Instead of allowing the partisan divisions of our culture to simply bleed over into the pews, what if the church became a place where we were committed to having honest, respectful, face to face (not digital) conversations about these issues that matter. The goal is not to change somebody else's mind, the goal is to build relationships, foster community, learn from each other, and have civil dialogue in a culture that has resorted to echo chambers of the like-minded. The goal is to gain a deeper realization that there continues to be far more that unites Christians than divides us. We must get to a place where we grow tired of the same old fights and divisions, and we realize that internal bickering is keeping us from our mission of serving and healing a broken world that clearly has lots of problems, lots of fear, and lots of pain.

53. Two Versions of Christianity

Last Sunday, I took my five-year-old son to his first Titans game. He was very excited, and we arrived early as I was curious to see what would happen during the national anthem. To my surprise neither the Tennessee Titans nor the Seattle Seahawks came out of the locker room until after it was over. The sidelines remained empty. That same day, *The Washington Post* ran a fascinating article by Michael Frost about two NFL players, Tim Tebow and Colin Kaepernick, neither of whom are currently playing in the NFL. They are both Christians and both famous for kneeling before football games but for very different reasons. Tebow is a conservative evangelical, homeschooled by Christian parents, and he spent many summers working alongside his missionary father in orphanages. He is pro-life, supports abstinence outside marriage, and is a popular speaker at evangelical conferences. In many ways, he is a golden boy for conservative Christianity and would pray to God for strength before the game. Kaepernick made a name for himself last year when playing for the Forty-Niners when he decided to start taking a knee during the national anthem. Born to a nineteen-year-old single mother and given up for adoption, he too is a Christian and credits his faith as the motivation for his activism and philanthropy. This decision turned him into one of the most polarizing figures in all of sports. Some can't stand him. Others praise him. When asked why he decided to start kneeling, he responded: "I am not going to stand up and show pride in a flag for a country that oppresses black people and people of color. To me this is bigger than football and it would be selfish on my part to look the other way." He has stood in solidarity with the Black Lives Matter movement and has spoken out against police brutality and racial injustice. His decision to kneel was certainly a controversial position that has offended many veterans who have fought to keep this country free.

In his article, Frost goes on to say that these two players represent two very different versions of Christianity present in our culture that do not seem to understand each other. He explains, "One values personal piety, gentleness, respect for cultural mores and an emphasis on moral issues like abortion, homosexuality, and another that values social justice, community development, racial reconciliation, and political activism. One version is kneeling in private prayer. The other is kneeling in public protest. One is concerned with private sins like abortion. The other is concerned with public sins like racial discrimination. One preaches a gospel of personal salvation. The other preaches a gospel of political and social transformation." For those of us who have been around the faith for a long time, these two versions of Christianity are nothing new. Kaepernick's version has its roots in the Social Gospel Movement of the early twentieth century (Walter Raushenbush). Tebow's faith stems from the more conservative tradition of Christianity that has grown in recent decades (Billy Graham) while mainline denominations have rapidly declined. What many seem to be missing here is that a complete understanding of Christianity involves both dynamics: "Love God with your heart, soul, mind, and strength. Love your neighbor as yourself."

It's not an either/or scenario. Many liberal Christians are guilty of only focusing on social activism and progressive politics. Many conservative Christians forget that Jesus stood in solidarity with the poor and the marginalized of his day.

At some point, our culture needs to evolve into an appreciation that the Christian faith is a big tent, with many denominations, traditions, politics, cultures, and ideologies. Tebow and Kaepernick are simply visible examples of a divide that has been present for many years.

54. When Christians Miss the Mark

Years ago, I was in Grand Lake, CO eating lunch at a restaurant when a guy walked in wearing a black T shirt with bold white letters saying, "JESUS, PLEASE SAVE ME FROM YOUR FOLLOWERS!" A seminary student at the time, I appreciated his humor. In my years as a pastor, there have certainly been times when I felt the exact same way. Not all those who claim to follow Jesus truly understand what he was all about. Many Christians fail to act Christ-like. NT Wright says this in his book *Simply Jesus*: "Jesus of Nazareth poses a question and a challenge two-thousand years after his lifetime: Who exactly was he? What did he think he was up to? What did he do and say, why was he killed, and did he rise from the dead? The challenge is likewise fairly simple: since he called people to follow him, and since people have been trying to do that ever since, what might 'following him' entail? How can we know if we are on the right path?" As we grow older, we often find ourselves with more questions than answers. That doesn't mean we doubt our faith, it just means we recognize the complexities and challenges of life.

We live in a culture where judgment, superficiality, proof texting, and binary thinking often prevail: we tend to view things as liberal or conservative, rich or poor, successful or unsuccessful, right or wrong, black or white. But the truth is, there is a lot of grey in life. Not everything fits neatly into a box. However, there are clear themes that emerge when we look at the life and teachings of Jesus. The first theme is love: loving God, loving neighbor, and treating others the way we hope to be treated. Love is perhaps better understood as a verb and not just a noun. But ours is a world full of people who don't feel loved, cared for, or even recognized. The second theme is that of compassion and mercy which emanates from love. There is pain and hurt all around us. People are hurting for many reasons, and Christ calls us to help. The world can be a competitive, shallow, cold, lonely place which is why we need each other. A third theme is forgiveness. Jesus taught forgiveness because for human beings who can and do hurt each other, it is a recipe for survival. Some of us carry far too many burdens from the past, and we refuse to let go. Resentment, anger, bitterness, and envy will damage the soul. A fourth theme is courage in the face of fear. We've entered an age of anxiety where fear is out of control. But Jesus says, "Be not afraid." We can worry ourselves to death over things that may never happen, and we miss the present moment. Finally, we find the theme of peace: "My peace I leave with you, my peace I give to you, I do not give to you as the world gives." It all begins with inner peace and then grows from there. Yet, many remain at war in their own heart. Without peace in our hearts, there will never be peace in our community or peace in our world. Ghandi famously said that he would have been a Christian were it not for all the Christians. He saw a clear disconnect between Jesus and many of his followers. Perhaps the guy at that restaurant in Colorado felt the same way.

55. The Future of Christianity in America

Many speculate as to whether the Church in North America will continue to decline and ultimately go the way of Europe. Dr. Frank Drowota, the founding pastor of Woodmont Christian Church (est. 1943), once said he dreamed of a church that would, "interpret truth in terms of the times, but challenge times in terms of the truth." Yet for many Christians today, there is clear disagreement as to when we should "interpret" and when we should "challenge." Many are now asking, "What is the church willing to stand for? Does it have the courage, conviction, and backbone to speak out to a constantly changing culture? What are the essentials?"

These are certainly fair and relevant questions. The authority, interpretation, and context of scripture is hotly debated among scholars and ministers. Swiss theologian Karl Barth, perhaps the greatest theologian of the twentieth century, became deeply concerned with the church's apathy and collaboration with Hitler's Nazi Germany, and for good reason. Both liberal and conservative scholars draw heavily on his *Church Dogmatics*. According to Duke New Testament professor Richard Hays, "Barth's prevailing concern was that if we conceive of ethics as the application of general principles to specific situations, we will in the end indulge our own wishes and whims, all the while claiming religious—or even biblical sanction. If so, we have poured the dictates and pronouncements of our own self-will into the empty container of a formal moral concept, thus giving them the aspect and dignity of an ethical claim (although, in fact, it is we ourselves who will them)." When Jesus was asked which law is the greatest, we know how he responded: "Love the Lord your God with all your heart, soul, mind, and strength. And, love your neighbor as yourself." Yet we also acknowledge that Jesus gave specific instruction on issues that Christians continue to debate—adultery, divorce, marriage, taxes, retaliation, war, wealth, greed, possessions, and lust just to name a few. No doubt, the American Church and those of us who actively support it find ourselves in challenging times. Many now refer to our age as "post-Christian" or simply "secular," but what exactly does that mean?

French philosopher Alex de Tocqueville visited this nation back in the nineteenth century to find out what made America great. He was surprised and offered these powerful insights: "I sought for the greatness and genius of America in her commodious harbors and her ample rivers—and it was not there . . . in her fertile fields and boundless forests and it was not there . . . in her rich mines and her vast world commerce—and it was not there . . . in her democratic Congress and her matchless Constitution—and it was not there. Not until I went into the churches of America and heard her pulpits aflame with righteousness did I understand the secret of her genius and power. America is great because she is good, and if America ever ceases to be good, she will cease to be great."

56. Predicting the Future of the Faith

There is constant speculation and anxiety continues in our culture about the future of American Christianity and the role of the church in the coming years. What will the faith look like ten, twenty, or fifty years from now? Why will some churches be forced to close their doors while others in the same zip codes thrive and grow? Nobody holds a crystal ball, but all ministers and Christian leaders should think about these questions because the decisions we make now play a big role in shaping and molding the future. These decisions will also determine whether we are able to reach our children and grandchildren with the values of Christianity. I offer the following twelve predictions about the future:

1. Denominational loyalty will continue to wane. There will be ongoing movement between Baptist, Methodist, Presbyterian, Episcopalian, non-denominational etc. Christians will be more concerned about being a part of a community where they can connect and grow spiritually than simply maintaining family loyalties to a particular denomination or congregation.

2. The words of Jesus will matter much more than creeds, doctrine, theologies, and hierarchies. Since the faith is built on Christ and his teachings, his words will matter most. Christians need to know and reflect upon what he said and did.

3. Churches will need to offer different styles of worship and music. Healthy churches will recognize that not everybody

worships the same way. Worship wars accomplish nothing. If your church is limited to one style or approach to worship, you are limiting your reach.

4. Mission and service must be a priority, and getting people involved in "hands on" mission will make all the difference. Writing checks is important but being hands on is transforming. The CEO who travels to Guatemala, Africa, or Appalachia will be changed and find incredible joy and purpose.

5. Small groups will continue to be the key to effective discipleship, relationships, and spiritual formation. New leaders must be recruited and trained. This is where genuine connections are made and life is lived.

6. Bold, visionary, and courageous leadership will be essential. The churches that do well will have both pastors and lay leaders who are always looking to the future, pushing the envelope, and willing to try new things. The seven last words of the church are, "We've never done it that way before."

7. Hospitality and authenticity will be essential. Warm and welcoming churches that are authentic, energetic, and genuine will do well. Nobody wants to be ignored when they come to church.

8. The church must be a place where genuine healing takes place. Judgment makes this difficult. There is a lot of pain and brokenness, and people need a place to heal and be honest. Recovery ministries, twelve step programs, divorce care, counseling, and spiritual growth all matter.

9. Church communities must work to become welcome alternatives to the polarization, division, and incivility that is defining our culture. This does not mean everybody agrees on politics or social issues, but we must work harder to listen and respect differences. If this does not happen, churches will simply mirror our polarized culture.

10. A consumer approach to Christianity (What can you do for me?) needs to be replaced with a servant form of Christianity (How can I serve?). One is self-centered, the other is selfless.

11. Websites, podcasts, and blogs will be a way of getting people in the door but cannot replace authentic community. Technology is important but has limits. Many people are now lonelier than ever.

12. Experiencing God (heart) will be much more important than knowledge about God (head).

57. Inner Peace in a Busy World

During the Season of Advent, I often talk about three different levels or kinds of PEACE: GLOBAL PEACE—which is certainly a challenge and is very complex; LOCAL PEACE— Or peace in our families and in our communities and our immediate surroundings: And INNER PEACE—or peace within our hearts.

I have come to the realization that all of these are interconnected, but they all start with inner peace. There will never be local peace and there will never be global peace until there is first inner peace, and for some reason, we live in a world where lots of people lack inner peace. This Advent season, I've found myself thinking about why that is. Why is there a prevalent lack of inner peace in our world and culture today? Why are so many people unhappy and unsatisfied? There are obvious answers to this question: growing anxiety, fear, regret, jealousy, envy, dissatisfaction, addiction, disease, mental illness, despair, grief, loneliness, insecurity, financial struggles. The list is very long and very familiar.

One of my favorite passages of scripture is found in John's gospel, the 14th chapter. Jesus says, "The Advocate, the Holy Spirit, whom the Father will send in my name, will teach you everything, and remind you of all that I have said to you. Peace I leave with you. My peace I give to you. I do not give to you as the world gives. Do not let your hearts be troubled, and do not let them be afraid."

In the Bible, the ancient word for peace is "shalom." And shalom never means the absence of trouble. It means that which makes for our highest good. The peace that the world offers to us is very different from the peace that Christ offers us. The peace that the world offers to us is an escape, an avoidance of trouble and difficult times. It's a day at the spa, a walk in the park, or a vacation. But the peace that Christ offers to us is the peace of conquest, the peace that allows us to deal with anything that may come our way in life. Nothing can take this peace away from us once we have it. It is an inner peace that is completely independent of outward circumstances and situations. It is a peace that we find, in God and it allows us to deal with all our worries and fears, all our trials and tribulations, all our uncertainty and insecurity, all of our doubt and uneasiness.

This world can and will throw many things at us - things that will test us, things that will hurt us, things that will knock us down, things that will set us back. But if we have the peace of Christ in our hearts, this world does not have control over us, because it is a peace that we find within, and it cannot be taken away. The frantic pace of our world keeps us constantly on the go, always interrupted, never satisfied, and never fulfilled. Christ fills the void that nothing else can, and at Christmas, we all long and pray for that peace in our hearts. Hopefully once we find it, that peace can extend beyond Christmas.

58. Who Is Jesus of Nazareth?

Methodist Bishop Will Willimon wrote a book a few years ago titled, *Why Jesus?* Willimon asks, "Do you want to see Jesus? Do you want to see the one who came from dry, dusty Galilee, moved under the cold gaze of peasants, a man destitute, without a job, house, or welcoming family? Do you want to see this one who, though he had nothing, refused to act like a submissive, cringing simpleton but stood up to the presumed powerful and dared to speak directly for God, tackling sickness and death and taxes head on, facing down both demons and swaggering, sword-wielding bullies? Do you want to see this one who, though he appeared so ordinary, made such wild, reckless claims for himself, reaching out to the dead, the dying, and the demented? Do you want to see this one whom we dare to believe is God with us? If so, then come and see."

Jesus means different things to different people, and our culture has a hard time agreeing on exactly who Jesus is what he calls us to be and to do.

For some, he is simply a historical figure of the past.
For others, he is living and real.
For some, he is the rubber stamp on conservative politics and ideologies.
For others, the driving force behind liberal policies.

For some, he brings up bad memories of a very rigid upbringing.
For others, the memory of a loving church home that nurtured them in their early years.

For some, he is a symbol of intolerance.
For others, he is a symbol of inclusivity and welcome.

For some, he is challenging and inspiring.
For others, he is just an obligation at Christmas and Easter.
For some he is life changing
For others, he is life draining.

Whatever we think about Jesus, we can all agree that he is a fascinating figure who has changed the course of history and who wants to change our lives today if we are up for it. In Luke's gospel, Jesus is baptized by John the Baptist in the Jordan River, and he then escapes to the wilderness for forty days by himself where he is tempted. Later, he begins his Galilean ministry in the synagogue by reading these words from Isaiah: "The spirit of the Lord is upon me because he has anointed me to bring good news to the poor. He has sent me to proclaim release to the captives and recovery of sight to the blind, to let the oppressed go free, to proclaim the year of the Lord's favor."

Luke then tells us that he rolls up the scroll, gives it back to the attendant, sits down and says, "Today this scripture has been fulfilled in your hearing." From these prophetic words that Jesus chooses as his "inaugural address," we can gain a lot of insight into his agenda and his priorities. We can begin to understand who he was and what he came to do. He cared deeply for the poor, he helped the blind to see again, and he freed the captives. And guess what? We are all captives to some degree. It might be economic captivity, and in Jesus's day, the poor were being exploited in many ways. But captivity can be defined as anything that keeps us from fullness of life: fear, worry, anger, depression, addiction, regret, jealousy, materialism, love of money, racism, bigotry, pride, death, grief - you name it. Jesus came to free us from these things.

We find ourselves enslaved to unhealthy relationships where we are emotionally and sometimes even physically abused. Enslaved to debt, credit card bills, and the money that we owe from buying things that we really shouldn't have bought in the first place because we couldn't afford them. Many people are enslaved to their own situations or circumstances in life. Some are held captive by depression and mental illness, and they just can't seem to get rid of that dark cloud that constantly hangs over their heads. Some are held captive by loneliness, and they are looking for just one other person in life who genuinely cares about them and who loves them. Many of us are aware of certain things that we do in life that are unhealthy. We are aware that we overeat, over-drink, and overspend. We know that we worry too much, but we cannot seem to stop. We know we work too much, but we just can't seem to cut back. And oftentimes, we keep on going down the same road even though we know we shouldn't.

Maybe it's time we meet Jesus Christ again in a new and healthier way and let him free us from our captivity. Maybe it's time we let go of religious baggage and some things in life that continue to hold us back. Maybe it's time we follow Jesus' lead and open our hearts to the presence of God.

59. Not Your Ordinary King

Former Bishop of Durham and well-known New Testament scholar N.T. Wright has authored a new book entitled *Simply Jesus*. Wright is one of the most widely read and highly respected scholars in his field. In the very first chapter of the book entitled, "A Very Odd Sort of King," he tells how Jesus did not fit the mold or expectations that many had for a king in that day.

> "They were looking for a builder to construct the home they thought they wanted, but he was the architect, coming with a new plan that would give them everything they needed, but within a new framework. They were looking for a singer to sing the song they had been humming for a long time, but he was the composer, bringing them a new song to which the old songs they knew would form, at best, the background music. He was the king, all right, but he had come to redefine kingship itself around his own work, his own mission, his own fate" (Wright 5).

To this day, many of us still struggle to identify exactly who Jesus was and is, what he did and did not do, and we are guilty of underestimating the many ways that he continues to challenge and transform our lives today. A genuine relationship with Jesus is anything but boring and mundane.

We must remember that Christianity is not about an institution or a certain creed, a doctrine or a particular theology. It's not about ecclesiastical hierarchies or church politics. It's not about picking the right denomination or preacher. It's not about having power, or numbers, or money, or getting your own way. Christianity is all about developing and nurturing a personal relationship with Christ that is ongoing, and we either have it or we don't. Or maybe we have it, but we just haven't paid much attention to it recently. Maybe we have neglected it. Maybe we have been distracted by too many other things.

We are all guilty of letting other things crowd out our faith. We are all very good at making excuses as to why we can't follow. We have mastered it. We are too busy, too preoccupied, too booked up, too important, too scared, too comfortable. We are over committed and spread too thin. Maybe all of our allegiance is to a politician or a political party, or to a church or a preacher and that keeps us from stopping and responding to Jesus' call, asking us to love, to forgive, to turn the other cheek, to be generous, to look out for those who have little or nothing. So many times, we will follow, but only if it is convenient for us; only if it is on our terms; only if we can fit it into our schedule.

There are many in our world today who try to monopolize Jesus and put him in a box. They claim to have figured him out once and for all. They claim to know everything about him. The truth is, we will spend a lifetime coming to know this amazing man from Nazareth. We will spend a lifetime reflecting upon the Sermon on the Mount, studying the parables, being challenged by his teachings about wealth and money, being dazzled by his healings, and pondering what it means to welcome the Kingdom of God into our hearts and our lives. He is a fascinating person because he is the Son of God, and just when we think we have him figured out once and for all, our eyes and hearts are opened once again!

60. Jesus Still Speaks to our Modern World

Many will ask if Jesus is still relevant today. Some may say, "He lived two thousand years ago in ancient Palestine when they thought the world was flat and coming to an end, how can he help me in 2014?" Consider this: In a world where the arrogant and popular seem to get all the attention and the most aggressive often get their way, Jesus says, "Blessed are the poor in spirit, for theirs is the Kingdom of God."

Every single one of us suffers loss and grief, loneliness and regret. He says, "Blessed are those who mourn, for they will be comforted."

People are often dishonest, manipulative, and passive aggressive. He says, "Blessed are the pure in heart, for they will see God."

In an age of war, hostility, rivalry, and division, where fear and a need for control often lead to conflict. He says, 'Blessed are the peacemakers for they will be called children of God."

While we often forget the influence we have on others, he says, "You are the salt of the earth. You are the light of the world."

Adultery is far too common, ripping families apart. He says, "Watch your thoughts: whoever looks at a woman with lust in his eyes has already committed adultery in his heart." In other words, be careful what you think about because thoughts lead to actions.

Often, we don't just get mad, we want to get even. He says, "Turn the other cheek."

We are guilty of turning the people who have hurt us into enemies. He says: "Love your enemies and pray for those who persecute you."

While many give to charity for the recognition, the praise, the social status and prestige, he says, "Give your alms in secret, and your father who sees in secret will reward you."

Many are overtly pious and want others to see how faithful they are. He says, "Pray in secret and don't use empty words. Forgive others, if you want God to forgive you."

We are obsessed with accumulating wealth and possessions, constantly checking the market as our main source of security in life. He says, "Don't store up for yourselves treasures on earth. Store up treasures in heaven. You cannot serve both God and wealth."

We spend so much of our time and energy worrying about everything under the sun—our health, our reputation, our job, our security, our investments, our marriage, our children, our grand-children, the future, and even death itself. He says: "Do not worry about your life, what you will eat or what you will drink. Or about your clothing, what you will wear...Can any of you by worrying add a single hour to your span of life? Don't worry about tomorrow. Today's trouble is enough for today."

We are often all guilty of judging other people based on their skin color, class, possessions, age, gender, marital status, reputation, wealth, and connections. He says, "Do not judge, so that you may not be judged. Why do you see the speck in your neighbor's eye but do not recognize the log in your own eye? Take the log out of your own eye then you can see clearly the speck in your neighbor's eye."

We are often lost, confused, and perplexed. Yet he says, "Ask and it will be given to you. Search and you will find. Knock, and the door will be open to you."

We are often rude, hostile, inconsiderate, and lack civility.

He says, "In everything… do unto others as you would have them do unto you." These principles are so simple, so profound, yet so challenging. I would reserve the possibility that these words may be more relevant today than ever before.

61. Moving Beyond Fear-Based Faith

Popular Patheos blogger Benjamin Corley recently published a new book titled *Unafraid: Moving Beyond Fear Based Faith*. Corley grew up in an ultra-conservative, hell-fire and brimstone tradition where sin, judgment, and the wrath of God were pivotal parts of the theology. Years later, he suffered a mid-life spiritual awakening. He asked himself, "Why would God seek to punish and torture his creation? Why are so many Christians taught that we are undeserving, inadequate, and damned?" It no longer made sense in his mind. He was over it, and he's not alone. Many in our culture have had it with the concept of a judgmental God who has it out for his people. If you doubt that, check out the empty pews. It simply doesn't square with the teachings and message of Jesus Christ. Corley finally decided, "We can hold a fear-based foundational understanding of God or a love-based understanding of God, but we cannot hold both: love doesn't fear, and fear doesn't love." For the hard core biblical literalists, there is clearly a scriptural basis for this: "Let us love one another because love is from God. Everyone who loves is born of God and knows God for God is love." The passage continues, "There is no fear in love but perfect love casts out fear" (I John 4). So why is there still so much fear in religion? Corley answers, "I think our experience of Christianity, and religion in general, is usually rooted in fear because religions are designed to address the one fear we all hold in common: death." Fear has been the mechanism through which religion and many religious leaders have sought to control the people. But the evidence shows that people have grown weary of it. There is enough fear in this world without religion making it worse.

What people are hungry for is what Jesus taught: hope, love, compassion, forgiveness, empathy, peace, and truth. Religion with a future must be part of the solution and not part of the problem. Does that mean that anything goes? Of course not. Decisions have consequences. Humans have free will. But when faced with whether to live a life of fear or a life of love, love is the better choice. Love is what the world needs. Love is what Jesus taught. People are tired of being afraid. They are tired of worrying about what "could or might" happen tomorrow. Henri Nouwen says, "When we begin to understand at a deep, spiritual level that we live surrounded by love and in communion with God no matter what the external circumstances, we can let go of the fear that lurks on the outskirts of our minds." Prayer is key in this process. For Corley, it was an intentional decision to change but one that was long overdue. It opened up an entirely new world. He explains, "Making the conscious decision to reject a fear based God is the floodgate that leads us to experience not the loss of faith but freedom from fear-based faith in order to discover a truer and deeper faith." We must face the harsh reality that people in this culture are simply tired of living in fear. And healthy religion helps us to face it and move beyond it.

62. Peace that Lasts

As we move beyond Christmas, take down the tree, and prepare to begin a New Year, we often experience disappointment when returning to a post-Christmas reality. It's back to a world that is anxious, fearful, stressed, and overcommitted. It could be called a materialistic rat race where everybody is trying to keep up with everybody else, and we are never satisfied. It's a world of competition, comparison, envy, jealousy, and wanting what others have. But at Christmas, the Prince of Peace called us away from all that because it keeps us at war with ourselves and at war with each other. Jesus says, "My peace I leave with you. My peace I give to you. I do not give to you as the world gives." Is it possible to hold on to the peace of Christmas as we look ahead to 2015? I would hope so.

Peaceful people understand the transforming power of forgiveness. All of us has been done wrong. Somebody has hurt us, offended us, disrespected us, or ignored us. We all have that in common. Jesus taught forgiveness. Christians are good at talking about forgiveness but struggle to forgive. Forgiveness doesn't mean you forget, but it does mean that you let it go. Forgiveness doesn't mean that you set yourself up to be hurt again, but that you put your hurt in the past and move on. Forgiveness is not always easy but is always necessary. Peaceful people realize they can't control everything in life. Stanley Hauerwas, in *The Peaceable Kingdom*, says: "Our need to be in control is the basis for the violence of our lives. For since our 'control' and 'power' cannot help but be built on an insufficient basis, we must use force to maintain the illusion that we are in control." Some things in life are controllable, but many more things are out of our control. We must accept that reality. Peaceful people do not get sucked into unnecessary conflict with non-peaceful people. It always takes two to fight. If somebody is combative, manipulative, or passive aggressive, and you get tangled up with them, you then have to play by their rules, or you will lose. Many times, walking away is a much better option if possible. Jesus said turn the other cheek, go the extra mile. Peaceful people have also learned to be fully present in the moment. Somebody once asked a Zen Master what monks do, and he responded by saying, "We sit, we walk, we eat." The person then replied, "Well I also sit, walk, and eat, and I'm not a monk!" To which the Zen Master replied, "Yes, but when we sit, we know we are sitting. When we walk, we know we are walking. When we eat, we know we are eating."

We have now mastered the challenge of multi-tasking with the help of technology, but in the process, we have forgotten how to enjoy the moment. Most importantly, peaceful people have found peace with themselves. Those who are most combative, angry, and aggressive are almost always those who are not at peace with themselves, so they project it on to everybody else. This begs the question, "How do we make peace with ourselves?" It starts with prayer, forgiveness, acceptance, and gratitude and is a life-long endeavor. Inner peace will never be possible if we are at war in our own hearts, so here's to the peace of Christmas remaining in our hearts and lasting well into 2015.

63. Searching for Christmas Joy

We are only two days away from Christmas. I have discovered that the Christmas season is much like life in general. There is a lot going on, and many plans are being made. There are a multitude of activities, parties, people to see, cards to send, and gifts to buy. We experience many emotions—joy, happiness, sadness, sorrow, loneliness, exhaustion, grief, fear, compassion, hope, peace—all mixed together. For those with small children who believe in Santa, Christmas can be magical, full of excitement and wonder. Yet for those who have lost a spouse or family member and find themselves grieving or alone, Christmas can be difficult—excruciatingly painful. Christmas is a time to reminisce, to take a stroll down memory lane. We remember Christmases growing up, when our kids were young, when our parents were alive, when life seemed simpler. We think of friends who have come and gone and wonder what they are doing now.

The truth is, many of us live our lives the exact same way that we go through the Christmas season—very busy, very tired, stressed out, rushing around, distracted, in a hurry, not slowing down, not being quiet…and then we miss it. We turn around and we have missed it! Children have grown up and moved away. They've married and started their own families. Grandchildren are born. Parents have aged and maybe even passed on. Relationships have drifted apart. Christmas reminds us that life is full of change and it presses forward whether we want it to or not. If you're not careful, you'll miss it. But one truth remains. Whatever emotions you might be experiencing this Christmas, whatever has happened this year for good or bad, it is still possible to find joy.

Joy is different from happiness. Everybody wants to be happy, but nobody is happy all the time. Joy is much deeper, more meaningful, and resonates in the depths of our soul. Joy involves the acceptance of life the way it is, flaws, disappointments, and all. And joy can come when we least expect it. There are many things that try to stand in the way of joy—stress, worry, pain, fear, envy, anger, selfishness, loneliness, addiction. But these are simply human realities, obstacles that we must face and overcome.

We must learn to find joy in the ordinary, basic things. Stanley Hauerwas says it well in *The Peaceable Kingdom*, "The most remarkable aspect of learning to live joyfully is that we learn to see the simple and most common aspects of our existence, such as our friends, our spouses, our children, as sheer gifts to which we have no right but who are nonetheless present to us." Joy and inner peace go hand in hand. Nobody ever said that finding joy is easy, but in a world of constant noise, breaking news, never ending distractions, anger, and discontentment, we need to experience something different. The carol says, "A thrill of hope, the weary world rejoices." Yes, it's a weary world, but we stand ready to rejoice. It's still not too late to find joy this Christmas. It will only come when you are fully present with the people that you love and when you open your heart to the presence and mystery of God.

64. The Real Gifts of Christmas

The stores and malls are busy with shoppers looking for the perfect gift, but the gifts that we are all looking for cannot be bought or delivered by Amazon. Deep down in our souls, we all long for the spiritual gifts of hope, peace, joy, and love. We live in anxious times. Anxiety and fear have become the defining spiritual dilemma of the twenty-first century. In his book *My Age of Anxiety*, Scott Stossel says, "To some people, I may seem calm. But if you could peer beneath the surface, you would see that I'm like a duck—paddling, paddling, paddling." That resonates, even during this season of peace on earth, goodwill to all. Stossel says, "Being severely anxious is depressing. Anxiety can impede your relationships, impair your performance, constrict your life, and limit your possibilities." Physicians will now tell you that treating anxiety in both children and adults is an integral component of practicing medicine. Theologian Paul Tillich once said that all our anxieties and fears can be placed into one of three buckets: fear of death, fear of emptiness or meaninglessness, and fear of guilt or condemnation. Leadership experts have written countless books on how to lead and live in anxious times. Edwin Friedman talked about the importance of "self-differentiation." Peter Steinke talks about being a non-anxious presence, steady and calm in the midst of uncertainty. Ron Heifeitz talks about the importance of "holding steady" and learning to take the heat, whatever it may be. But for any of this to happen, we must first find our own sense of inner peace and joy that does not depend on other people or external circumstances.

Inner peace is a choice that we make. We must seek it

and then work to maintain it. If we wait for the external conditions of our lives to become perfect, it will never happen. Joy must become a mindset as we live from day to day. MIT professor Otto Scharmer identifies three voices that we battle in our minds. The first is the voice of judgment, which is intellectual, sealing off the mind to protect the status quo. The second voice is cynicism, which is born out of mistrust, telling us that everybody is out to get us, hurt us, and stab us in the back. The third is the voice of fear that keeps us afraid of losing what we have earned and accomplished. These are the same voices that keep us from experiencing joy. While we may not choose our circumstances in life, we all choose our attitude and response.

The Dalai Lama and Desmond Tutu identify eight pillars of joy: perspective, humility, laughter, acceptance, forgiveness, gratitude, compassion, and generosity. Each of these virtues is essential in the spiritual life. Buddha once said, "Peace comes from within, do not seek it without." But perhaps Meister Eckhart said it best: "Spirituality is not to be learned by flight from the world, or by running away from things, or by turning solitary and going apart from the world. Rather, we must learn an inner solitude wherever or with whomsoever we may be. We must learn to penetrate things and find God there." That is our challenge this Christmas and beyond.

65. Why Our World Needs Christmas

We all long for inner peace, but it's in short supply in our crazy culture. What is the evidence of this claim? Road rage, sexual harassment, incivility, anger, hostility, church shootings, nuclear threats, special counsels, opioid addiction, alcoholism, disappointment, envy, dissatisfaction, you name it. We see it every day on the news, and yes, the news has a vested interest in keeping us from inner peace. It gets old and wears us down. Has it always been this way? Perhaps, but probably not. Spiritual emptiness and restlessness is a growing universal disease. Harvard psychiatrist Armand Nicholi Jr. once wrote an article titled "Hope in a Secular Age." He says: "The cause of despondency in many today is an awareness of a gap between what they think they ought to be and what they feel that they are. There is a discrepancy between an ideal they hold for themselves and an acute awareness of how far short they fall from the ideal." I think Nicholi is correct. Many are not happy with their lives and remain restless and dissatisfied. Bad things happen. Setbacks occur. Pain is real. There is distance in relationships, distraction at work, and many long to be somewhere else.

What seems to be lacking is the peace that passes understanding. Christmas gives us a chance to find and hold on to inner peace, but it will not happen automatically. It takes work, intentionality, focus, and calm. Inner peace does not come from other people; it never has. Inner peace is an ongoing choice that we make to block out the noise, the craziness, the threats, the fear, and the expectations of others long enough to be still and present. Blaise Pascal famously said, "All of humanity's problems stem from our inability to sit quietly in a room alone." If we look to the world to find inner peace, we will not find it. Jesus said, "My peace I leave with you, my peace I give to you, but I do not give to you as the world gives." Inner peace must first be found in our hearts. Is this easy? No. Is it worthwhile? Yes. Human beings are masters of stirring up drama and conflict. That's a given. But we get to decide how to respond when somebody else hurts us, harms us, or does us wrong. We get to choose our words and our reactions. Thomas Jefferson concluded, "Nothing gives a person so much advantage over another as to remain always cool and unruffled under all circumstances." This certainly doesn't mean we are passive, indifferent, and uncaring. It simply means we have learned to control our emotions and reactions. Emotional intelligence is important.

What the world needs now are peacemakers, those who build goodwill and better friendships. What the world needs now is hope to counterbalance the negativity, fear, and cynicism. What the world needs now is more humility and less selfishness, more compassion and less narcissism, more grace and less judgment. All is not lost. But there is serious work to do. The golden rule is not golden to everybody. What do we really want this Christmas? Inner peace? Yes. Hope? Yes. Joy? Yes. But Amy Grant's words still hold true: "No more lives torn apart, and wars would never start, and time would heal all hearts. Everyone would have a friend, right would always win, and love would never end." That's why our world needs Christmas.

66. How Christ Saves Us

Palm Sunday begins the greatest week of the year for Christians. Jesus' decision to enter Jerusalem riding on a donkey fulfilled Zechariah's prophecy and was an emphatic statement of who he was: he was the messiah. But his kingdom and his message was one of peace and not war, one of love and not conquest. In first century Palestine, when a king would go to war, he would ride on a war horse, but when a king came in peace, he would ride on a donkey. Jesus was coming in peace. His message was a message of peace. His kingdom was a kingdom of peace. His life was a life of peace. His way was and still is the way of peace. And yet we still live in a very violent world with many Christians forgetting that they serve the Prince of Peace. Jesus' kingdom is still very different from the kingdoms of this world. The Kingdoms of this world are based on power and money, influence and status, intimidation and fear, force and violence. Jesus' kingdom is based on love and forgiveness, grace and reconciliation, peace and hospitality, humility and service. Throughout his life and ministry, he showed that he came not to destroy, but to love; not to condemn, but to help; not to judge but to forgive; not to divide but to unite. Yet we still have a hard time grasping what this kingdom looks like today because it is so different from the world in which we live. But we long for it. And we pray for it. And hopefully, we are working for it.

Peace is not just the absence of war, force, and destruction. Jesus also calls us to peace in our hearts and in our personal relationships, where we don't get angry, we don't get resentful, and we don't get worked up over little things. There are a lot of people in our world who are not physically violent, but who are emotionally violent meaning that they hate, they resent, they despise, they manipulate, and they are jealous. And these things do not lead to peace.

Palm Sunday reminds us that Jesus came to save us. "Hosanna" means "Save us now!" But how does Jesus save us today? Yes, he died on the cross. And there are many different theories of the atonement. But think about everything that he taught throughout his life and ministry.

He saves us from our selfishness.

He saves us from materialism.

He saves us from jealousy.

He saves us from lust.

He saves us from emptiness and meaninglessness.

He saves us from judging others.

He saves us from self-righteousness.

He saves us from power struggles.

He saves us from anger and rage.

He saves us from addictions.

He saves us from arrogance.

He saves us from fear.

He saves us from hopelessness and despair.

He saves us from fearing death.

He saves us from ourselves.

We need Jesus in our lives because he saves us from all these things that we struggle with each and every day. And the way that Jesus saves us is through the cross. The cross is a stark reminder to us of how the world often responds to his message: with rejection, ridicule, intolerance. Many still don't have time for it and still don't want to hear it. It's not convenient. It's not easy. It's not the way of the world. We still crucify his message.

67. Was Jesus Political?

Holy Week is upon us which causes me to wrestle with a question: "Was Jesus a political person?" If we look at the way his final days unfolded, we might get our answer.

Stanley Hauerwas says, "Jesus' triumphant entry into Jerusalem is an unmistakable political act. He has come to be acknowledged as King. He is the son of David, the one long expected to free Jerusalem from foreign domination. Yet this king triumphs not through violent revolt, but by being for Israel the one who is able to show it that its worship of God is its freedom. He is Israel's long expected priestly king whom the prophets said would come. His entry into Jerusalem is, therefore, rightly celebrated by those who are not in power."

Can you imagine the irony of Palm Sunday? The Jewish people were expecting a great warrior. They were expecting a mighty soldier to liberate them from Roman oppression. They were expecting a grand entry into the city similar to that of Pontius Pilate. And here comes Jesus, humble, calm, riding on a donkey, reminding us that the kingdom of God is very different from that kingdoms of this world.

What happens at the temple? He gets angry at the money changers and causes a scene. He turns over the tables and quotes Jewish scripture by saying, "My house shall be called a house of prayer, but you are making it a den of robbers." Hauerwas says, "Going to the temple is perhaps even more significant than his triumphant entry into Jerusalem. The temple defines Israel. The worship of God and political obedience are inseparable. The abuses surrounding the temple and Israel's political subjugation are but aspects of the same political reality." Rome had figured out the best way to occupy the land: paying the Jewish religious leaders well to keep the people in line. The chief priests had sold out for financial gain.

According to N.T. Wright, "Jerusalem had lost its way so drastically; somehow the leaders of the Jewish people had gotten things so wrong in their collusion with Rome and in their corruption, oppression, and greed; somehow the Jewish people, Jesus' own people, had gotten things so wrong in their determination to bring God's victory to the world through military violence and armed rebellion—that the only word the last of the prophets can now speak is the word of judgment found in Matthew 24: 'Not one stone will be left standing upon another. All of them will be thrown down." Jesus showed incredible courage in calling out the authorities, but he knew it would not end well. He knew that you can't challenge the system without dire consequences. We know what happened Friday.

Wright says, "That is part of the mystery of his crucifixion: 'wounded for our transgressions, crushed for our iniquity.' He cannot establish the new creation without allowing the poison in the old to have its full effect. He cannot launch God's kingdom of justice, truth, and peace unless injustice, lies, and violence do their worst and, like a hurricane, blow themselves out, exhausting their force on this one spot. He cannot begin the work of healing the world unless he provides the antidote to the infection that would otherwise destroy the project from within." It all comes together Holy Week. "We see how the early work of Jesus' public career, the healings, the celebrations, the forgiveness, the changed hearts all look forward to this moment. This is what it looks like when Israel's God becomes king." Jesus showed incredible courage. What about us?

68. Polarization is not Christ's Will

So far the twenty-first century has been marked by on-going polarization within the Christian community. Christians have proven time and time again that we are very good at fighting with each other. This causes many to leave the church and dismiss organized religion. The night before he was crucified, Jesus prayed that "all would be one so that the world might believe." At what point will the church and our society understand the need for civility and faithful disagreement over controversial issues? Many will say that the church has ignored its real mission in order to battle the culture wars. There could be some truth to that. Social issues seem to carry the day and overshadow many other important matters. Mike Slaughter, Charles Gutenson, and Robert Jones published a fascinating book in 2012 titled *Hijacked: Responding to the Partisan Church Divide* saying "Why is it, then, that we have allowed political partisanship to enter so deeply into our churches? And, perhaps more importantly, how is it that we have allowed those differences to divide us, to create obstacles among us, and to have created an environment in which one or the other can be somehow considered less a 'follower of Jesus' simply on the basis of one being the supporter of a particular party or ideology." It should be abundantly clear by now that discipleship, partisanship, and social positions do not line up neatly.

In his book *The Happiness Hypothesis*, social psychologist Jonathan Haidt shows that both liberals and conservatives make valuable contributions to society because of their different interests and passions. He writes, "My research confirms the common perception that liberals are experts in thinking about issues of victimization, equality, autonomy, and the rights of individuals, particularly those of minorities and non-conformists. Conservatives on the other hand, are experts in thinking about loyalty to the group, respect for authority and tradition, and sacredness. When one side overwhelms the other, the results are likely to be ugly. A society without liberals would be harsh and oppressive to many individuals. A society without conservatives would lose many of the social structures and constraints that Durkeim showed are so valuable." This is also the case in the case in the church, demonstrating the ongoing need for mutual respect and healthy dialogue among all groups. We can and should learn from each other.

Let's face it: we as Christians are perhaps as unsuccessful as any at being able to disagree passionately while still maintaining fellowship with those with whom we disagree. Many ministers desperately long for this to happen. We need to look for unity in the things essential to the faith. We need to allow diversity of opinion on things that are not essential and not be threatened by disagreement. But regardless of whether we agree or disagree on any given topic, Christ calls us to model love, civility, and decency for one another.

69. Faith, the Opposite of Fear

Dr. Stephen Diamond once wrote an article for *Psychology Today* titled *Essential Secrets of Psychotherapy: Why We Worry (and What We Can Do About It)*. Diamond sums up why we worry:

"We fear the future. The unknown. We worry about what will happen to us, our family, our spouse, our business, our money, our home, our possessions, our country, the world, etc. We live in a universe which is inherently unpredictable, dangerous and deadly. Indeed, anxiety (and the worry it generates which generates more anxiety) can be understood as an acute or subliminal awareness of life's insecurity. And the ever-present possibility and absolute inevitability of death. So much of what we worry about has to do with losing what we have: health, happiness, love, wealth, power, status, wisdom, freedom, independence, support, vitality and, ultimately, life itself. Existential anxiety is a recognition, either conscious or unconscious, that life is finite, existence tenuous, and that all or what little we have can be taken from us at any time."

We worry because life is fragile. We worry because bad things happen to good people. We worry because what we have worked hard to build can be taken from us in a moment, and that doesn't sit well. We worry because we think it will help us control things, but in reality, it doesn't.

In seminary, I encountered a book called *The Courage to Be* written by an existential theologian named Paul Tillich. In that book, Tillich identifies the basic difference between fear and anxiety. He says, "Fear, as opposed to anxiety, has a definite object which can be faced, analyzed, attacked, and endured." On the other hand, "anxiety" is fear that "has no object, or its object is the negation of every object." You could describe anxiety as fear of the unknown, and sometimes we can't identify exactly what we are afraid of we just know we're afraid.

In the gospels, we find Jesus telling us not to worry because worry is the opposite of faith. Worry is the opposite of putting our complete trust in God. It doesn't mean that we just sit back and give up, but we do our part, we work hard, we prepare, and then we leave the rest to God. We stop trying to control the uncontrollable—wisdom that lies at the heart of the Serenity Prayer. Too many of us think that we can control certain things that are outside of our control. Faith simply does not equal control. The writer of Hebrews says, "Faith is the assurance of things hoped for, the conviction of things not seen." (Hebrews 11:1).

There is a difference between saying that we trust in God and actually trusting in God. It's amazing how we will say that we trust in God for our eternal salvation, but so often we don't trust in God with our daily experiences of life. One of my favorite passages of scripture is I John chapter 4: "There is no fear in love, but perfect love casts out fear..." I love this verse because it is so very true, and all of us need to hear it over and over again. In the Sermon on the Mount, Jesus says, "Do not worry about tomorrow, for tomorrow will bring worries of its own. Today's trouble is enough for today." It was Jesus' steadfast belief that we should deal with each day as it comes and not become overly anxious about the future. And if we are able to do this, not only will our fear and anxiety subside, but we will allow ourselves to enjoy the present because if you think about it, the present moment is a gift. It's all that we have, so we should never take it for granted. Life is what happens to us while we're busy worrying and obsessing about the future. Life will pass us by if we're not careful.

So live life one day at a time. Be thankful for what you have, prepare for the future, but don't obsess about it. Your worries and fears will begin to subside.

70. *Don't live in Fear*

One powerful phrase is repeated twice in Matthew's Easter account that I think might be the best Easter sermon we can hear: "Do not be afraid." The angel says to the women, "Do not be afraid! I know you are looking for Jesus who was crucified. He is not here, for he has been raised." Jesus later appears to the women and says the exact same thing, "Do not be afraid. Go and tell my brothers to go to Galilee, and there they will see me." I think this might be the Easter message. Stop living in fear! Too many of us live our lives in fear every day—and it's no way to live.

Fear we're going to run out of money
Fear we might be abandoned
Fear that others will reject us
Fear our lives won't matter
Fear that our health won't hold up
Fear that our kids don't appreciate or respect us
Fear that our marriage isn't going to last
Fear that our country isn't the same it once was
Fear there are too many people moving into our town
Fear that our health is going to get worse and worse
Fear that our best years are now behind us
And yes, fear that one day we are going to die.

This is no way to live: afraid all the time. Anxious all the time. Worried all the time. Scared all the time. Nervous all the time. It takes the joy out of living, and it's not what God intends.

There is a great book titled *The True Measure of a Man* by

a guy named Richard Simmons (not the aerobics guy). Simmons says this about fear: "Fear is created by uncertainty over the future, even if the ultimate outcome has only the slightest potential to be negative. Fear can produce a complexity of emotions. It can be a powerful force for taking positive action in our lives, or it can produce potentially crippling emotions." Unfortunately, much of the fear in our culture falls in the second category. It paralyzes people—leaves them scared to death and it takes the joy out of life.

Fred Craddock recently passed away. Although he stood just over five feet tall, he was a preaching giant. He once concluded an Easter sermon this way:

"You see, the opposite of faith is fear. Fear is death is itself. Why don't you go out for the ball team? Afraid I won't make it. Why don't you try out for the school play? Afraid I won't get the part. Why did you lie to your parents? I was afraid of punishment. Why did you cheat on the test? I was afraid I would fail. Why were you so jealous? I was afraid of losing love."

Craddock says, "Afraid, afraid, afraid, afraid, afraid, afraid. That's the refrain of what we are and what we do. But don't be afraid. Don't be afraid to live and love and laugh. Don't be afraid to give and serve and care. Don't be afraid to speak and do. That's the message of Easter. Don't be afraid. Don't be afraid. For he said, 'I'll be with you always. Even to the end of the world.' That's Easter!

IV

SPIRITUALITY

71. The Spiritual Challenge of Being Human

Human beings are complicated creatures. We have the capacity to love others by showing mercy, compassion, forgiveness, and grace. We also have the capacity to be ugly, rude, short, and mean. We have the capacity to serve others and to do goodness, love kindness, and walk humbly. And, we have the capacity to be selfish, hateful, and arrogant. How do we explain it—this battle that goes on inside? Sin? Brokenness? Pride? Paul writes to the Romans, "I don't understand my own actions. For I do the very thing that I hate." We can all relate.

In *The Road To Character*, David Brooks talks about Adam I and Adam II and how we all have both within us, even if one dominates the other. "Adam I is the career-oriented, ambitious side of our nature. Adam I is the external, resumé Adam. Adam I wants to build, create, produce, and discover things. He wants to have high status and win victories." Brooks says Adam I is focused on success and accomplishment, status and prestige. He explains, "Adam II is the internal Adam. Adam II wants to embody certain moral qualities. Adam II wants to have serene inner character, a quiet but solid sense of right and wrong—not only to do good but to be good. Adam II wants to love intimately, to sacrifice self in the service of others, to live in obedience to some transcendent truth, to have a cohesive inner soul that honors creation and one's own possibilities. While Adam I wants to conquer the world, Adam II wants to obey a calling to serve the world. While Adam I is creative and savors his own accomplishments, Adam II sometimes renounces worldly success and status for the sake of some sacred purpose."

The truth is, we live in a world that glorifies Adam I, but our faith is forever calling us to let Adam II come out. Our world is competitive, fast, cruel, materialistic, and busy. Adam II grows weary of all these things. Many people do not come to terms with Adam II until the second half of their lives, perhaps even later. Many books have been written about this: Bob Bufford's *Halftime* and Richard Rohr's *Falling Upward* are two that come to mind. In 1997, Thomas Keating gave a series of lectures at Harvard Divinity School titled "The Human Condition." He said, "We spend the first part of our lives finding a role—becoming a mother or father, a professor, a doctor, a minister, a soldier, a business person, an artisan, or whatever. Whoever we think we are, we are not. We have to find that out and the best way to find that out, or at least the most painless way, is through the process that we call the spiritual journey. This requires facing the dark side of our personality and the emotional investment we have made in false programs for happiness and in our particular cultural conditioning."

The spiritual journey is not easy, but it is absolutely necessary. It is life-long, filled with ups and downs. For each of us to come to terms with the dark side of his personality is both difficult and humbling. Jesus asked, "Why do you see the speck in your neighbor's eye but fail to recognize the log in your own eye?" The spiritual journey begins when we embrace our own shortcomings and then do our best to love, serve, and create peace in this broken world.

72. Seven Enemies of the Heart

Most people believe that the spiritual life matters. Even those who reject organized religion will tell you that they believe in the importance of spiritual growth and formation. However, we live in challenging times where there are many obstacles to achieving spiritual growth and inner peace. These obstacles need to be named because in many ways, they serve as "enemies of the heart." The first obstacle is FEAR. We live in a culture of fear, and politicians use that fear to control us. Fear keeps us in a state of uncertainty because we never know what might happen next. Fear can be crippling and even paralyzing, sucking away our quality of life and our ability to enjoy the present. The second obstacle is ANGER, which seems to be the direct result of fear. In a highly polarized and contentious culture where partisanship has become toxic and even deadly, anger is real. We see it all around us. Einstein once said that, "Anger dwells only in the bosom of fools." Emerson said, "For every minute of anger, you lose 60 seconds of happiness." But Aristotle put it best: "Anybody can become angry—that is easy. But to be angry with the right person, and to the right degree and at the right time and for the right purpose, and in the right way—that is not within everybody's power and is not easy." Acting out in anger is usually a bad idea. The third obstacle is ENVY, much of it resulting from major socioeconomic divides within the culture.

Arthur Brooks of the American Enterprise Institute once said "We must recognize that fomenting bitterness over income differences may be powerful politics, but it injures our nation. We need aspirational leaders willing to do the hard work of uniting Americans around an optimistic vision in which anyone can earn his or her success. This will never happen when we vilify the rich or give up on the poor." Envy is a dangerous road to travel because there is always somebody who has more. Envy is often the result of ingratitude and a lack of contentment. The forth obstacle is LUST. Lust has destroyed many marriages and families and decisions that are made in just a few short moments can have life-long consequences. Lust has become even more common in a culture that glorifies sex and ignores boundaries. The fifth obstacle is RESENTMENT. Failure to forgive and let go of the past keeps many people in unnecessary bondage. Some are better than others at letting go of the past. The sixth obstacle is NEGATIVITY. Psychologists have confirmed that our brains tend to automatically remember negative situations and criticism, but it takes a more concentrated effort to focus on what is good and positive. Negativity becomes a downward cycle, and there is nothing worse than two negative people feeding off each other. The final enemy of the heart is MATERIALISM, turning to things to satisfy spiritual longings. This is age old, but it never works. Of course, we all enjoy nice things, but houses, cars, clothing, jewelry, and money do not satisfy our deepest spiritual hunger. That hunger can only be satisfied by God, relationships, love, and acceptance.

73. Who Are the "Spiritual but not Religious"?

"I'm spiritual but not really religious." This is the new mantra of our age. I hear it all the time. You probably hear it. For some reason, people don't seem to have a problem with spirituality, but there are many stereotypes and preconceived notions about organized religion and church. Some of them are accurate and some of them are not, but these stereotypes are certainly present. Younger generations are open and honest about their feelings on this subject.

Harvard theologian Harvey Cox says that we have now entered the AGE OF THE SPIRIT. It began roughly 60 years ago and in it, doctrine and creeds are not nearly as important as breaking down barriers between religions and denominations. Now we see non-denominational churches sprouting up and growing all over the place. Cox says that in this era, spirituality is replacing formal religion and actually experiencing the divine is much more important than maintaining correct beliefs. Cox says that spirituality can mean many different things. It is the rejection of pre-packaged theological propositions. It is an attempt to voice the awe and wonder of creation and life and how that can not just be limited to within the church walls. And spirituality realizes that we have a lot to learn from both inter and intra religious dialogue, learning from other religions and learning from other Christians.

In her book *Christianity After Religion*, Diana Butler Bass identifies what she sees as the difference between the two. She says that for many in our culture, RELIGION is associated with institution, organization, rules, order, dogma, authority, beliefs, buildings, structure, defined principles, hierarchy, boundaries, and certainty. SPIRITUALITY, on the other hand, is associated with experience, connection, transcendence, searching, intuition, prayer, meditation, nature, wisdom, inner life, 12 steps, inclusivity, and doubt. Which of the two sounds more appealing? The challenge for many churches is that many people are failing to grow spiritually within the walls of the church. Bass says, "On Sundays, other things are more interesting: *The New York Times*, shopping, sports, Facebook, family time, working in the garden, hiking, sipping lattes at Starbucks, the dog park, and kids sports." Ask any pastor and they will tell you this is real.

74. Reaching the "Spiritual but not Religious"

We now find ourselves living in an age where many consider themselves "spiritual but not religious." There are many reasons why people feel this way: church is boring; they've been hurt by organized religion; there's a clear disconnect between Jesus and those who claim to follow him; there are alternative ways to find community; there is a lack of trust in religious institutions; people have used the church to push a specific political agenda. It is common knowledge now that the fastest growing religious group in our culture are the "nones"—those not affiliated with any faith tradition. Many of the "nones" consider themselves spiritual and hungry for community.

In his profound book *The Future of Faith*, retired theologian Harvey Cox says that Christianity is drastically changing. He identifies three basic eras in the history of Christianity. The first era he calls the AGE OF FAITH. This was from the time of Jesus until the rule of the Emperor Constantine in the fourth century. In this age, he says that the church was more concerned with following Jesus' teachings than enforcing what to believe about Jesus. The second era he calls the AGE OF BELIEF. This era began when Constantine made Christianity the official religion of the Roman Empire. It spread drastically and quickly. During this time, the church focused on orthodoxy and correct doctrine and asked the question, "What are we supposed to believe about Christ?" We have now entered the third and final era, according to Cox, and it is called the AGE OF THE SPIRIT. It began almost 60 years ago, and in this era, doctrine and creeds are not nearly as important as breaking down barriers between religions and denominations. Now, denominational loyalty is not what it used to be. Cox says that in this era, spirituality is replacing formal religion, and having a personal experience with the divine is much more important than holding correct beliefs or quoting scripture. Cox says that spirituality can mean many different things. It is the rejection of pre-packaged theological propositions. It is an attempt to voice the awe and wonder of creation and life and to express how that cannot be limited to within the church walls. And spirituality realizes that we have a lot to learn from both inter- and intra-religious dialogue, learning from other religions and learning from other Christians.

Many will ask, "what does this mean for the future of the church?" That's an important question. It means that the church must be intentional about helping the younger generations grow in their spiritual lives and not get too bogged down with the baggage that organized religion often carries. Here is what matters most: growing spiritually, mission, outreach, service, relationships, changing lives, a living relationship with Christ, and the experience of authentic community. Here is what doesn't matter as much: denominations, budgets, creeds, hierarchy, non-functioning committees, church politics, and ecclesial hierarchies. Young believers are looking for a faith that is authentic, life changing, and relevant to their lives. Faith communities that seek to grow and remain vibrant in the 21st century should take note because, according to Cox, the age of the spirit is here to stay.

75. Experiencing God

Nashville has hockey fever! The Nashville Predators have the entire city behind them in search of the Stanley Cup. Bridgestone arena and lower Broadway are rocking. Last Sunday at the back door of church, I was asked, "Wouldn't it be great if people would get as excited about Jesus Christ as they are about the Nashville Predators?" That's an interesting question. Even Joel Osteen can't get that kind of energy in an arena. NYU Social Psychologist Jonathan Haidt argues that human beings are tribal. We ban together through sports, politics, religion, race, nationality, and culture. Loyalty to the tribe is very important. Haidt would say that for many people, sports serves as a form of religion, a form of worship. It creates an instant bond and is an emotional experience.

One of the reasons many young people give for not being interested in the church is that they view it as boring. Compared to the many other options in our entertainment culture, many millennials look at church as dull, irrelevant, and out of touch. This is especially a challenge for many aging mainline congregations that are experiencing sharp declines in membership and giving. From my perspective, churches facing the greatest challenge are the ones that neglect spiritual formation and have low energy. Energy is contagious and plays a very important role in religious life. Enthusiasm literally mean "God within." Healthy religion touches both the head and heart and leads to an authentic experience of God. Community plays an important role in this. Simply knowing about God is not enough. Experiencing God is where real transformation takes place. For many, this will require a drastic theological recalculation, and some are not up for the task. Many prefer to put God in a neat little box, but that is not possible. What does this mean for the church today and the future of Christianity? It means that the church must help the younger generations grow in their spiritual lives and not get too bogged down with the baggage that organized religion likes to carry. The church must show how Christ can transform our lives, give us purpose, and lead us out of a mundane and meaningless existence. Young believers are looking for a faith that is authentic, life changing, and relevant to their lives. They are looking to truly experience God and to from meaningful relationships.

76. Anxiety, Depression, and Our Spiritual Crisis

Social isolation, loneliness, anxiety, and depression continue to be growing challenges in the twenty-first century. Harvard sociologist Robert Putnam first pointed this out almost twenty years ago in his groundbreaking book *Bowling Alone: The Collapse and Revival of American Community.* The Internet and now social media were born into a culture where traditional forms of community were breaking down due to various societal factors. In a new book called *Lost Connections: Uncovering the Real Causes of Depression and the Unexpected Solutions,* journalist Johann Hari makes the case that the rising rates of anxiety and depression in our culture may not simply be tied to chemical imbalance in the brain. He is not completely dismissing that possibility, but he is arguing that there are multiple life factors that have contributed to this rise, all related to Putnam's original argument of communal fragmentation.

In writing the book, Hari talked to multiple psychologists around the world who have done extensive research on the subject of anxiety, depression, and social connection, including neuroscience researcher John Cacioppo. "Caciopppo told me the evidence is clear: social media can't compensate us psychologically for what we have lost—social life. More than that—our obsessive use of social media is an attempt to fill a hole, a great hallowing, that took place before anyone had a smartphone." Clearly, big tech companies found a way to tap into this void and have made billions of dollars in the process. Folks like Jobs and Zuckerberg realized that this is both a spiritual crisis and a relationship crisis. But are we any better off now that we have all these gadgets and social media platforms? Many would say the situation is even worse because screen time is no substitute for the authentic community that has traditionally been found in churches, civic clubs, PTA's, and twelve step groups. Hari also points out that as our society has become less communal and more fragmented, our culture has become more materialistic. Why? It's the way we compete and send messages of status and importance to others.

There is a common belief that we can spend and consume our way to happiness, but it never works. There is always more to get. Hari consulted American psychologist Tim Kassar who has done extensive research in this area. Kassar concludes, "All of us have certain innate needs—to feel connected, to feel valued, to feel secure, to feel we make a difference in the world, to have autonomy, to feel we are good at something. Materialistic people are less happy because they are chasing a way of life that does a bad job of meeting these needs. What you really need are connections. But what you are told you need in our culture is stuff and a superior status, and in the gap between those two signals—from yourself and from society - depression and anxiety will grow as your real needs go unmet." One of the questions Hari asks in the book is, "If anti-depressants are the answer to anxiety and depression, then why do so many people who take these medications remain anxious and depressed?" He believes that there is much more to the situation than simple brain chemistry. Life experience, social isolation, and loss of connection all plays a role. And it might be time for our culture to wake up and recognize that simply popping pills cannot be the only answer.

77. Our Elusive Search for Happiness

I once heard a well-known minister from California say the following words emphatically: "Spiritual emptiness is a universal disease." How do we know that this is true? Take a look at our culture. Look at the rising levels of depression, anxiety, loneliness, alcoholism, drug addiction, anger, fear, hate, and incivility. Each of these things points to rising levels of spiritual emptiness and a culture that needs spiritual renewal and revitalization. This is not to paint a completely pessimistic and dismal picture of where we are. Many are able to find healthy ways to nurture their souls and tend to their spiritual lives. However, there are clear indicators that many struggle to find meaning, are less fulfilled, and more restless than ever before. Certain factors are causing this including the fast pace of our culture which is largely driven by technology. We don't take time to slow down and reflect. It is also caused by our failure to nurture the soul. In the same way that our physical bodies need exercise, diet, and sleep, our soul also has fundamental needs. These include stillness, prayer, reflection, connection, and quality time with those whom we love and who care deeply about us. There is a clear correlation between our spiritual well-being and our ability to find happiness.

In his book *Happiness: The Art of Living with Peace, Confidence, and Joy*, businessman Doug Smith says, "Happy people have an underlying sense of well-being and contentment. They remember the past with peace, anticipate the future with confidence, and experience and live in the present with joy and exuberance. This attitude is sourced by a life integrated by meaningful purpose and sound principles and enhanced by healthy relationships and appropriate pleasure." It is important to note that Smith chooses the word "happiness" as a broad term that incorporates meaning and purpose. The quest for human happiness is certainly nothing new. 2000 years ago, Aristotle said, "Happiness is the meaning and the purpose of life, the whole aim and end of human existence." Jesus of Nazareth said, "I came that they may have life in all of its fullness." When signing the Declaration, our nation's founders said that we all have God given rights to "life, liberty, and the pursuit of happiness." However, in this ongoing pursuit, there are common misunderstandings which include: the belief that money buys happiness; fame and status bring happiness; and that possessions can fill our deepest yearnings. All of these things are false. Money might bring some security but not lasting happiness. Jim Carrey recently said, "I wish everybody could be rich and famous, so they could discover how empty it is." Happiness at its core is tied to spirituality and fulfillment. We must discover and value the things in life that truly give us meaning. Blaise Pascal argued that the only way to find happiness is to uproot false beliefs and replace them with genuine wisdom. This involves replacing fear with faith, cynicism with hope, false friends with genuine relationships, anger with forgiveness, and jealousy with gratitude. Spiritual emptiness happens when we focus on the wrong things, and we all do it. The only remedy is to focus on the right things. Or as Paul the Apostle writes, "Whatever is true, honorable, just pure, pleasing, commendable, excellent, and worthy of praise." This is what deserves our time and attention.

78. Three Theories of Happiness

Every human being longs to be happy, but we all recognize that happiness is fleeting. It comes and goes. One day we are up, the next day we're down. One day we are on top of the world, the next day, the world has run us over. Our founding fathers said that we have a God-given right to life, liberty, and the "pursuit" of happiness. Everybody enters this pursuit very differently. In his book *The Happiness Hypothesis*, NYU social psychologist Jonathan Haidt identifies three different theories of human happiness. The first theory is the "progress principle:" happiness comes from success and acquiring things. This is the principle that dominates our consumer culture. We feel that we will be happier if we make more money, buy a nicer car, a bigger house, or more toys. However, the author of Ecclesiastes figured out just how disappointing this mindset can be when he writes: "Then I considered all that my hands had done and the toil I had spent in doing it, and again, all was vanity and a chasing after the wind." (Ecc 2:11) Time and time again, we find that the person with the most toys is still not happy or content. The second theory is the one most common in Buddhism and other eastern religions. "Buddha, Epictetus, and many other sages saw the futility of the rat race and urged people to quit. They proposed a particular happiness hypothesis: Happiness comes from within and it cannot be found by making the world conform to your desires." The goal here is to move away from desire and attachment because it inevitably leads to suffering. Meditation, contemplation, and yoga are common ways to achieve this. This approach involves trying to not control the uncontrollable. There is great wisdom here.

This theory also recognizes the shallowness and superficiality of our materialistic culture. There will always be something newer, shinier, and better to buy. Haidt concludes that both of these theories are inadequate and he proposes a third theory that he believes is the most convincing: happiness in life comes from between. "Happiness is not something that you can find, acquire, or achieve directly: you have to get the conditions right and then wait." The conditions to which he is referring have to do with relationships: "relationships between yourself and others, between yourself and your work, and between yourself and something larger than yourself." Once we are able to get these relationships right, happiness will come. However, in the process, there are certain things that will make this difficult. The Dalai Lama and Desmund Tutu refer to these as "obstacles to joy" that every human being must navigate: stress and anxiety, frustration and anger, sadness and grief, loneliness and despair, envy and jealousy, suffering and adversity, illness and the fear of dying. Being aware of these things is important. They must be replaced with perspective, humility, humor, acceptance, forgiveness , gratitude, compassion, and generosity. For Jesus, the heart of all of this is love, compassion, and living the golden rule. If we can focus on these things, our relationships in life we be in a healthy place.

79. Convenient Substitutes for God

Ralph Waldo Emerson once said, "A person will worship something, have no doubt. That which dominates our imaginations and our thoughts will determine our lives, and our character. Therefore, it behooves us to be careful what we worship, for what we are worshipping we are becoming." Tim Keller writes: "What is an idol? It is anything more important to you than God, anything that absorbs your heart and your imagination more than God, anything you seek to give you what only God can give. A counterfeit god is anything so central and essential to your life that, should you lose it, your life would feel hardly worth living." There are plenty of idols and counterfeit gods in our lives that we turn to for security and meaning on a regular basis. The most common include: 1) SELF. Many think life revolves around them and are only concerned with their own needs. The concept of putting others first does not even begin to cross their mind. Christians are called to deny self in the midst of a selfish culture. 2) MONEY: Friedrich Nietzsche once predicted that western culture would soon replace God with money. To a large degree, he was right. We live in a world where it's all about money. Those who don't have any money want more and those who have plenty fear losing it. There are very few things in our world that motivate people like money. To some degree, it's understandable because it takes money to pay for basic necessities in life like food, shelter, clothing, and education. But misunderstandings about money abound in our culture. It does not solve all problems. If it's true that wealth brings about ultimate happiness and satisfaction, then shouldn't the wealthiest people in our culture today be the happiest and the most satisfied? Jesus didn't say you can't be wealthy. He said, "You cannot serve both God and wealth."

3) SOCIAL STATUS: We want to know the right people, be in the right place, go to the right parties, send our kids to the right schools, have the right connections. We treat certain people differently if we think they will help us climb the ladder, but Jesus didn't seem to be too concerned about social status. He challenged authorities. He hung around the rich and the poor. Sometimes, we're way too concerned about it.

4) PHYSICAL BEAUTY: It's amazing how much time and money we will spend trying to make ourselves look young and beautiful. Many people are much more concerned with outer beauty than inner beauty. Remember, the Lord looks on the heart.

5) CHILDREN: Many parents give their children everything they want, protect them from failure at all costs, but forget that their primary role is to be their parents first, and not just their buddies.

6) MATERIAL THINGS - Houses, cars, TV's, furniture, designer clothing, shoes, purses, hand bags, jewelry, watches - all the things that we think we have to have to keep up, to be happy and satisfied, but the joke is always on us. We get this stuff, but it never satisfies us. We always want more.

7) POLITICS: When partisan politics from either side get in the way of logic and sound decision making, we have a problem. Sometimes we are so blinded by political ideology that we refuse to think for ourselves.

8) WORK: Usually our intentions are good, but we can quickly lose our sense of balance and find ourselves living to work rather than working to live. Rarely will you hear somebody on his death bed say, "I wish I had spent more time at the office."

9) DRAMA & CONFLICT: There are some people in life that thrive on drama and conflict. They are always out to pick a fight. If everything is going well, if it's a peaceful time, then you don't see them. Living in community and interacting with other people is not always easy. But the more peaceful and understanding we can be, the better. God speaks to us through the Ten Commandments: "You shall have no other gods before me." The Israelites made a golden calf. How are we doing?

80. Obstacles to the Spiritual Life

You may recall a cover story that appeared in *Newsweek* magazine about three years ago. It was written by Andrew Sullivan and was titled, "Forget the Church, Follow Jesus." The subtitle of that article was "Christianity has been destroyed by politics, priests, and get rich evangelists." In that article, Sullivan identifies the scandals and corruption that have given organized religion a bad name. But he does identify something that is very important, and research has proven it to be true: people in this day and age are much more interested in following Jesus Christ than they are in getting caught up in the details of an institution. He identifies Thomas Jefferson and St. Francis of Assisi as being two men that were very serious about their faith and their spiritual lives. At the end of the article, he says this: "True Christianity comes not from the head or the gut, but from the soul. It is as meek as it is quietly liberating. It does not seize the moment; it lets it be. It doesn't seek worldly recognition, or success, and it flees from power and wealth. It is the religion of un-achievement. And it is not afraid. In the anxious crammed lives of our modern, twittering souls, in the materialistic obsessions we cling to for security in recessions, in a world where sectarian extremism threatens to unleash mass destruction, this sheer Christianity, seeking truth without the expectation of resolution, simply living each day doing what we can to fulfill God's will, is more vital than ever...." And he concludes by saying, "Something inside is telling us we need radical spiritual change."

We live in a busy, stressful, fast paced world, and we all know that. Recently, I've been giving lots of thought to the primary factors in life that keep us from being spiritually centered. Here are just a few:

FEAR—fear of things that may or may not happen. One of Jesus' primary messages was "Be not afraid." It's hard to be spiritual when you're always afraid.

RESPONSIBILITY—We all have various responsibilities in our jobs, in our marriages, and with our children and families. Just taking care of the things that we are supposed to take care of can make spirituality difficult. The things that called me into the ministry—a desire to preach, teach, counsel, heal—are not necessarily the things that I spend all of my time doing. Administration is not very spiritual. Handling conflicts is not very spiritual, yet these are responsibilities that we have.

CONFLICT—There are people in life who just like to fight, and they are always creating conflict. This usually says more about what is happening in their own hearts than it does about the source of the conflict itself.

EGO and CONTROL—wanting our lives to matter. Wanting to be important. Wanting others to recognize how great we are. These things don't always help us live spiritually.

POSSESSIONS—as much as we love our possessions, we have to admit that sometimes they end up possessing us. And so our stuff often gets in the way of being able to live a spiritual life.

These are just some of the obstacles that we must deal with and overcome to grow spiritually. Eliminating these things is not possible or even desirable. But navigating them and finding balance is important if we are to experience the peace that Christ gives.

81. The Loneliness Challenge

Nebraska Senator Ben Sasse has a brand new book out titled *THEM: Why We Hate Each Other and How To Heal.* You might be under the impression that this book is simply about politics and polarization but it goes much deeper than that. He actually focuses on one of the greatest challenges of the twenty-first century: loneliness and its devastating effects on our society. We might ask, "How can this be? Aren't we connected more today than ever before with smart phones, the internet, and multiple social media platforms." That's the delusion but its false. Sasse says, "At first glance, it might seem that technological breakthroughs promise to mitigate our social capital deficit. It turns out that at the same time any Billy Bob in Boise can broadcast his opinions to thousands of people, we have fewer non virtual friends than at any point in decades. We're hyper connected and we're disconnected." Simply put, social media is an inadequate substitute for authentic connections. In fact, it might be exacerbating the problem.

Sasse, a former college president who holds a Ph.D. in history from Yale, points out the difference between social isolation and loneliness. Social isolation happens when a person objectively lacks relationships. But loneliness is much broader or more devastating. "According to psychologists, loneliness includes the inability to find meaning in one's life." This is the same concept that Johann Hari identifies in his recent book *Lost Connections.* Losing meaningful connections with family, friends, and meaningful work often leads to despair and depression. Loneliness is clearly tied to our nation's current opioid epidemic. Sasses points out that

Americans consume almost all of the world's hydrocodone (99%) and most of its oxycodone (81%). In the United States, roughly 116 people die every single day from opioid related drug overdose. People are trying to escape the misery and it is literally killing them. Loneliness is becoming the defining spiritual challenge of the twenty-first century. So what's the answer? Let's start with what the answer is not: social media. Social media is a shallow substitute for authentic relationships and is clearly more of a problem than a solution. It has become another form of addiction. However, it's here to stay, so it must be tempered and limited, especially among children.

The answer is community and healthy relationships. The answer is a return to the social connections that once made our communities strong: friendships, family dinners, neighborhood parties, book clubs, church, synagogue, small groups, and coffee shops where people actually talk to each other. The answer is found in learning to deny self and looking to serve the needs of other people. The answer is found in having conversations where we actually listen, empathize, and aren't always rushing off to the next thing. The answers seem obvious, but for some reason, are challenging in this new age. Sasse says, "There is a growing consensus that the number one health crisis in America right now is not cancer, not obesity, and not heart disease—it's loneliness. And with our nation's aging population, it's only going to get worse." The challenge for our culture is to return to basic human interaction, starting within the family, and not just the ones that happen on a screen.

82. Unintended Consequences of Secularization

One of the greatest challenges for people of faith in the 21st century is a growing secular culture. This happened in Europe decades ago, and many predict it is now happening in the U.S. Philosopher Charles Taylor says it well in his book *A Secular Age*, "The change I want to define and trace is one which takes us from a society in which it was virtually impossible not to believe in God to one in which faith, even for the staunchest believer, is one human possibility among others." He says, "Belief in God is no longer axiomatic. There are alternatives. And this will also likely mean that at least in certain milieu, it may be hard to sustain one's faith." One problem with secularism is that it often takes over our lives before we realize it.

Belief in God and a commitment to faith and spiritual practice get pushed aside and are replaced by things that may not necessarily be bad in and of themselves (family, sports, work). I once asked Stanley Hauerwas what he thought the greatest challenge would be for Christians in the 21st century, and he responded with one word: idolatry. It is ironic that the first two commandments are: 1) You shall have no other gods before me. 2) You shall not make for yourselves an idol. Secular culture tries to persuade us that there is no ultimate reality, nothing transcendent, nothing divine. It lures us into a commercial rat race of consumption and consumerism, competition and comparison, a shallow game to see who can collect the most toys in the shortest amount of time. Secular culture is full of egos and idols and leaves us obsessed with the opinions of others. Tim Keller poses the question this way: "What is an idol? It is anything more important to you than

God, anything you seek to give you what only God can give. A counterfeit god is anything so central and essential to your life that should you lose it, your life would feel hardly worth living…It can be family and children, or career and making money, or achievement and critical acclaim, or saving 'face' and social standing. It can be a romantic relationship, peer approval, competence and skill, secure and comfortable circumstances, your beauty and your brains, a great political or social cause, your morality and virtue, or even success in the Christian ministry." Idols take on many forms and not all of them seem bad or problematic. In fact, many are good if kept in balance. The problem is that we lose perspective, and all our energy and devotion goes to them, and then they always disappoint. They never satisfy our deepest yearnings and desires.

Wisdom comes when we learn to see secular culture for what it is and then rise above it. It doesn't mean that we escape it, but we transcend it. Wisdom comes when we confront our egos and insecurities so that we can surround ourselves with people who have spiritual depth and compassion. If we are unable to do this, the secular culture will eat us alive, keep us restless, and leave us devoid of meaning and fulfillment.

83. The Danger of Anger

Robert Schuller, former minister of the Crystal Cathedral in Los Angeles once referred to the seventh beatitude, "Blessed are the peacemakers," by saying this: "Do you want peace in your family? Do you want peace in your community? Do you want peace in other races and other cultures? There will not be peace anywhere as long as there is a war going on in your heart and in your soul." What does it mean to be at peace in our hearts and in our souls?

For some reason, we live in a culture where there is a lot of anger. There are a lot of people that are not at peace with themselves. And what's sad is that many people don't know that they're angry or why they're angry. They're just angry with a big chip on their shoulders. Anger always comes out at some point, but usually at the wrong time and towards the wrong person.

Albert Einstein once said, "Anger dwells only in the bosom of fools." Ralph Waldo Emerson said, "For every minute of anger, you lose 60 seconds of happiness." And it was Aristotle that said, "Anybody can become angry—that is easy. But to be angry with the right person, and to the right degree and at the right time and for the right purpose, and in the right way—that is not within everybody's power and is not easy."

Doctors will tell you that anger can lead to high blood pressure, incredible stress, and the inability to focus and relax. It can also lead to heart attacks, strokes, and even cancer. Physical symptoms of anger include headaches, stomach aches, rapid heart rates, shaking or dizziness. Emotional symptoms include being sad, depressed, guilty, resentful, or anxious. Anger has also been known to make people sarcastic, to take away their sense of humor, cause them to raise their voice, and even drive them to drink or smoke excessively. Some people will turn to prescription pills to deal with anger—which is never a good thing. The bottom line is: anger greatly affects our health and our quality of life.

Jesus was very good at handling anger. In fact, there is really only one instance in the gospels that we find him acting out in anger, and that is when he drove the money changers out of the temple. He was upset that the house of worship was being used to take advantage of the poor, so he got angry. But besides this one situation, Jesus seemed to stay calm.

In the Sermon on the Mount, Jesus talks about the subject of retaliation. He says, "You have heard that it was said, 'An eye for an eye and a tooth for a tooth.' But I say to you, Do not resist an evildoer. But if anyone strikes you on the right cheek, turn the other also; and if anyone wants to sue you and take your coat, give your cloak as well; and if anyone forces you to go one mile, go also the second mile. Give to everyone who begs from you, and do not refuse anyone who wants to borrow from you" (Matt 5). With these famous words, Jesus is advocating the importance of self-control. Again, he reminds us that although certain things will happen that are out of our control, how we respond - or don't respond - to them is always in our control.

I love the story about a man named Jim who lived in a high-rise apartment building in New York City. He lived on the 15th floor, so every morning he would get on the elevator to take it down to the street level so he could walk to work. But most days, the elevator would stop on the fourth floor, and an old, bitter, unfriendly lady named Mrs. Taylor would get on the elevator.

"Good morning Mrs. Taylor," Jim would always say very enthusiastically, and she wouldn't look at him or say anything in return. This went on for several weeks. Every day that the elevator would stop on the fourth floor, Mrs. Taylor would get on and not respond to Jim's warm greeting.

Finally, one day after many of the neighbors had witnessed Jim repeatedly saying hello to Mrs. Taylor while getting absolutely no response, somebody followed Jim out of the elevator and said, "I don't understand. Why do you continue to greet Mrs. Taylor every morning when she refuses to say hello in return or even to look at you." To which Jim replied, "Just because her nature is to be cold and unfriendly, that doesn't mean that I need to change who I am."

84. A Prescription for Worry and Fear

Years ago, there was a group of psychologists who got together and made a list of what they called a time table of life's worries, which included the most common worries that people have at different stages of their lives. They said at age 18, we worry about ideals. At age 20, we worry about our appearance. At age 23, we worry about moral issues. At age 26, we worry about making good impressions on others. At age 30, we worry about our salaries and the cost of living. At age 31, we worry about having success in our business. At age 33, we worry about job security. At age 41, we worry about politics. At age 42, we worry about marital problems. At age 45, we worry about a loss of ambition in life. And then over the age of 45, they say that we tend to worry about our health, which only seems to get worse the more we worry about it. The truth is: we all have different worries at different stages of our lives.

In the Sermon on the Mount, Jesus says, "Do not worry about tomorrow, for tomorrow will bring worries of its own. Today's trouble is enough for today." This verse contains the secret for dealing with fear and anxiety in life: living life one day at a time. It sounds simple, but so many of us constantly fail to do it. We live in a culture where technology has now rendered us incredibly available yet unavailable in the present moment. In fact, we are unavailable because we are so available. We are constantly interrupted. We text, we email, we Facebook, we Tweet, but what we're not very good at doing (and it's getting worse with the younger generations) is being fully present in the moment. We're too distracted. We are too preoccupied. We are obsessed with multi-tasking.

Jesus is challenging us to be present, and to live life one day at a time, which also means one moment at a time. This is the key to the spiritual life. He says, "Today's trouble is enough for today." Don't worry about tomorrow. It will bring its own problems, but you can't deal with them, until they come. And remember, anxiety is fear of the unknown, and it runs rampant in our culture. Many of us are not sure what we are afraid will happen tomorrow. We just know we are afraid, and it keeps us on edge and awake at night. Jesus addresses this subject plain and simple. Do not worry. You cannot change or accomplish anything by worrying, so stop doing it. You're only ruining the present.

Western culture has not mastered this concept of living in the present. We don't do it very well. If there is one thing that we can learn from Eastern religions, it's the concept of living in the present, appreciating the moment, finding joy in the simple things, taking life one day at a time. The Jews of the first century had a saying that went like this: "Do not worry over tomorrow's evils, for you know not what today will bring. Perhaps tomorrow you will not be alive, and you will have worried for a world which will not be yours." T. S. Eliot once said, "Where is the life we have lost in living?" This is something for all of us to think about.

V

POLITICS & AMERICAN CULTURE

85. Moral Foundations for Political Disagreement

To put it mildly, this is a bizarre presidential election (2016), a political circus of sorts. By the time November finally gets here, we will have heard and seen it all. The two major party nominees, Donald Trump and Hillary Clinton have high disapproval ratings. Trump has never held elected office before, and some of the things that come out of his mouth are simply astounding. Many don't trust Hillary and believe she should have been indicted by the FBI. Trump is running against the establishment to shake up a broken and corrupt Washington. Hillary embodies the establishment having served as First Lady, a US Senator, and then Secretary of State. It seems as though many people will be making a decision this year to either stay home or simply vote "against" someone in this election. Why is there such profound political disagreement in this country? Why the hostile partisanship and polarization? How did we get to this point? Whatever happened to civility and mutual respect among public servants who simply disagree on tax rates, the economy, entitlements, social issues, and foreign policy?

The research of NYU social psychologist Jonathan Haidt has been very helpful in recent years. He is one of the few intelligent people shedding rational light on our current predicament in a fair and balanced way. He started as a political liberal in academia but later became a centrist, a moderate, also known as an endangered species. In his first book *The Happiness Hypothesis* he says, "My research confirms the common perception that liberals are experts in thinking about issues of victimization, equality, autonomy, and the rights of individuals, particularly those of minorities and non-conformists. Conservatives on the other hand, are experts in thinking about loyalty to the group, respect for authority and tradition, and sacredness." In his second book, *The Righteous Mind*, Haidt expands his claims to address the five moral foundations for politics: Care vs. Harm, Fairness vs. Cheating, Loyalty vs. Betrayal, Authority vs. Subversion, and Sanctity vs. Degradation. He suggests that a combination of family origin, socioeconomic status, life experience, social pressure, views of fairness, and personal priorities shape our moral and political worldview. According to Haidt, the political left is much more concerned with the Care/Harm and the Liberty/Oppression foundations, hence the emphasis on social justice and economic equality. This was certainly a theme throughout the DNC in Philadelphia. The political right, he says, can appeal to all five foundations. It holds a different view of liberty and people who espouse these beliefs want to be left alone, viewing liberal programs as the government trying to intervene in private life and take care of groups they care about, regardless of cost or efficiency. This theme was present at the RNC in Cleveland. Haidt says that one of the most basic questions in a political cycle is "whether to preserve the present order, or change it?" Trump says, "the world is falling apart and is becoming more dangerous every day." Hillary says, "There are problems but it's better than you think."

Given recent events (Paris, Orlando, Nice, etc.), the world is a very stressful and dangerous place. Extremist ideologies are present and ready to strike. It is also a complex world, full of opinions, disagreement, and a never-ending cycle of contentious rhetoric and hot issues. The age of digital media now allows people to type things they might never say to somebody's face. Morality is anything but simple because good, honest people disagree on how to see the world and how to fix the world. We all see things through our own lens. We are then drawn to people who see the world the same way we do. Haidt concludes one chapter of *The Righteous Mind* by saying this: "Morality binds and blinds. It binds us into ideological teams that fight each other as though the fate of the world depended on our side winning the battle. It blinds us to the fact that each team is composed of good people who have something important to say." Are people still capable of thinking for themselves or do they simply carry the party line? Also, does anybody place an emphasis on the importance of civility and dialogue? For the sake of our nation, let's hope so.

86. Freedom, Bondage, and the American Way

This weekend, we celebrate the 240th birthday of our great nation, a nation built on liberty, freedom, and justice for all. But what is freedom? Throughout history, many brilliant leaders and philosophers have given their own thoughts and definitions of freedom. Albert Camus once said that, "Freedom is nothing but a chance to be better." Thoreau said that, "All good things in life are wild and free." Dwight D. Eisenhower stated that, "We seek peace, knowing that peace is the climate of freedom." Noam Chomsky remarked that, "Democracy and freedom are more than just ideals to be valued - they may just be essential for our survival." A Greek historian once stated that, "The secret of happiness is freedom, and the secret of freedom is courage."

We live in a great country that prides itself on the concept of freedom, and this time every year we celebrate that freedom. We should be grateful and never take it for granted. Our founding fathers once stated that all men are created equal, and we all have a God-given right to "life, liberty, and the pursuit of happiness." But I will be the first to tell you that while we are fortunate enough to live in a free nation, many Americans simply don't live their lives as if they are truly free. Yes, we enjoy certain rights and privileges. But, I would argue that many of us are not as free as we'd like to be from day to day. In a "get it now" culture, expenses often exceed incomes. Many people are enslaved to the situations into which they were born and can't seem to get out. Some live in poverty and don't make enough money to feed their children and provide for their families. Some have more than enough but their spending habits are out of control. Some are enslaved to depression and mental illness, and they just can't seem to get rid of that dark cloud that constantly hangs over their heads. Some are enslaved to loneliness, and social isolation. They are looking for just one other person in life who cares about them and who loves them. Some are victims of senseless crime and hate, like we saw in Orlando, which then deprives them of many years of life and opportunity.

The reality is that in this great nation that we all love, freedom is not as simple as it might seem. When it comes down to it, the way that we often live our lives indicates that we really aren't as free as we believe. The spirit is willing, but the flesh is weak. We're in bondage and need to break loose. Twelve step programs figured this out a long time ago and have helped millions. What good is political freedom if it is not accompanied by spiritual freedom?

87. Understanding the Left and the Right

Winston Churchill is often attributed with saying, "If you're not a liberal at twenty, you don't have a heart, but if you're not a conservative at forty, you don't have a brain." That could be a dangerous yet exciting way to begin a lively dinner conversation in mixed company. Admittedly, I have a fascination with the various factors that tend to make people "liberal" or "conservative," fully realizing that these two words are loaded and often defined differently. As a pastor, I find this especially interesting as it relates to preaching, teaching, and maintaining harmony within the church. Our culture seems much more concerned with stances on the "issues" and less concerned with the thought process, dialogue, and life experiences that lead to those stances.

The research of NYU social psychologist Jonathan Haidt has been illuminating in this area. In a book titled *The Righteous Mind: Why Good People Are Divided by Politics and Religion*, Haidt expands his claims to address the five moral foundations for politics: Care/Harm, Fairness/Cheating, Loyalty/Betrayal, Authority/Subversion, and Sanctity/Degradation. He suggests that a combination of family origin, socioeconomic status, life experience, social pressure, views of fairness, and personal priorities shape our moral and political worldview. According to Haidt, the political left is much more concerned with the Care/Harm and the Liberty/Oppression foundations, hence the emphasis on social justice and political equality. The political right, he says, holds a different view of liberty and wants to be left alone, viewing liberal programs as the government trying to intervene to take care of groups they care about regardless of cost or efficiency. Neither has a monopoly on the truth. Haidt offers a definition of "ideology" as being "A set of beliefs about the proper order of society and how it can be achieved," with the most basic question being "whether to preserve the present order, or change it?"

Make no mistake, without these varying ideals and worldviews, the world would be a very boring place. Yet with them, we all acknowledge that the world is a very stressful place, full of opinions, disagreement, and a never-ending cycle of contentious campaigns and hot issues. Kindness and civility are absolutely necessary but often seem lacking. Morality is a complicated subject because good, honest people simply disagree on a multitude of topics. Haidt concludes one chapter of *The Righteous Mind* by saying this: "Morality binds and blinds. It binds us into ideological teams that fight each other as though the fate of the world depended on our side winning the battle. It blinds us to the fact that each team is composed of good people who have something important to say." I think he might be on to something here.

88. The Problem with Extreme Ideologies

Unfortunately, we now live in an age where extreme positions on both sides are dominating the headlines. As a reasoned moderate, I see this as problematic. Looking at our nation, there are at least five different ideological groups starting from left to right. Think of five circles in a row, but they are not all the same size. The NEO-LIBERALS have resorted to violence and even hate as a means of protesting policies of the current administration. Trees are being burned down in Berkley, and lectures are being cancelled on college campuses for safety concerns, reminiscent of the 1960's. The next group is the LIBERALS. They are not happy about the current state-of-affairs and are making their voice heard in a peaceful, direct manner. Then you have the CENTRISTS, who are basically being quiet and watching things unfold. Centrists have opinions, even passionate ones, but are slow to voice them. However, when they do speak, there is usually great wisdom and insight. Next you have the CONSERVA-TIVES. For many conservatives, Donald Trump was not their initial choice for president, but they chose him over the alternative because they didn't like the direction of the country. Conservatives may agree with and benefit from many of the policies put in place (tax policies, border control, etc.) even if they don't agree with the tone and rhetoric. Finally, you have the NEO-CONSERVATIVES. The neo-conservatives are extreme on the other side and seem to enjoy watching liberals and neo-liberals wallow in their misery. The problem many have with neo-conservatives is not just what they do but the manner in which they do it.

As I see it, the greatest challenge is with the extremes. The

Neo-Liberals and Neo-Conservatives antagonize each other and feed off of each other. They do not understand each other, nor do they seek to understand each other. The only hope for cooperation and compromise in our government and in our society will come from the inner three circles, which is where most Americans reside. This translates into a spiritual problem for our nation because the extremes keep everybody on edge. Fear and anxiety are pervasive. Resentment is present. Accusations abound. Friendships and families are strained. We are now at a point where many Americans do not want to watch the news nor do they know where to turn to find objective news sources that are not slanted and biased. In fact, the news feeds this ideological divide. Many say it will only get worse before it gets better. We will see.

Years ago, I learned about Aristotle's Golden Mean presented in his work "Nicomachean Ethics." It is a description of moral behavior as the mean between two extremes—at one end is excess, at the other deficiency. Find a moderate position between those two extremes, and you will be acting morally. This is what our world needs at this time. This is what our nation needs. This is what our churches need. Moderates need to speak up. An ongoing battle between extreme ideologies will not lead to a productive society. Truth can usually be found somewhere in the middle. Combine this with Jesus' timeless ethic of "do unto others as you would have them do unto you," and you have a pretty good starting point for how to live in the world.

89. President Trump's Spiritual Challenge

A year ago, very few Republicans or Democrats would have guessed that Donald J. Trump would be elected and sworn in as the forty-fifth president of the United States. What he has managed to accomplish, politically speaking, defied all odds and predictions. He proved political pundits and scientists to be dead wrong. He promised to shake things up and managed to connect with struggling Americans in ways that seasoned politicians of both parties simply could not. His administration is now underway, and an interesting one it will surely be: unpredictable, unscripted, and outside the box to say the least. David Brooks, not one of Trump's advocates, talks about the difference between resumé virtues and eulogy virtues. Resumé virtues are the skills that we bring to the market place, the things that we learn in school, the things that help us get jobs and progress in our careers. Resumé virtues are very important in terms of upward mobility and economic opportunity. Eulogy virtues are the things that preachers talk about at funerals, and these are not necessarily dependent upon resumé virtues. It's whether you are kind, loving, devoted to your family, compassionate, and a person of character.

Throughout his life, many would say that Donald Trump has managed to compile an impressive secular resumé. He's built a global real estate empire and made billions of dollars. He's bought hotels, resorts, casinos, and sky scrapers. He's become a name brand, a celebrity, and lives in a luxurious penthouse high above Fifth Avenue. He's been a reality TV star and has run Miss Universe Pageants all over the world. Now, he adds to that resumé, "President of the United States." He was elected by the people and has now been given the chance to do the job. Trump's challenge, it appears, will be a spiritual one, having to do with temperament, patience, faith, peacemaking, self-control, character, and bridge building. Some of his strongest supporters might even agree. The truth is, we all face this spiritual challenge, every day. It's part of being human. Some master it better than others. Trump will quickly realize that no president has the time, energy, or need to respond to every criticism that comes his way. When you study previous Presidents, from Lincoln to FDR, Reagan to Obama, it becomes clear that all of them were forced to develop a spiritual life, an inner sanctuary. The presidency not only ages you quickly but it drives you to your knees.

Up to this point, Trump has taken on the world like a one man wrecking crew. He is bold, tough, unafraid, and unapologetic. He has offended many while gaining a strong following in the process. However, the way Trump campaigned and even won the White House may not necessarily prove to be an effective method for leading the free world. Time will tell. Yes, Trump will be Trump, but he will soon discover why presidents age so quickly during their short time in office. The presidency will humble him, as it has done to those before him. And this is where his spiritual challenge will lie. He will have many opportunities to show compassion, mercy, forgiveness, and grace. The choice will be his to make. If he can rise to the spiritual challenge, he might discover what Alex de Tocqueville meant when he said, "the greatness of America lies not in being more enlightened than any other nation, but rather in her ability to repair her faults." Everyone is watching.

(Published January 20, 2017
on the occasion of Trump's Inauguration)

90. Living in an Age of Terror

Having now celebrated the 13th anniversary of September 11, 2001 with 13 years of war and bloodshed in Afghanistan and Iraq in the rear view mirror, we find ourselves with a growing new threat—ISIS. It appears as though the twenty-first century will continue to be defined by our ongoing struggle with religious extremism and hatred for the west and our way of life. The images we see in the Middle East are disturbing and can't be ignored. Innocent people including children are being beheaded, raped, and slaughtered. I have always had great respect for Duke theological ethicist Stanley Hauerwas who is famous for his pacifism. Although I don't personally agree with that stance, I believe that Hauerwas has wise words for us. I continue to be reminded of these words he wrote in an article after 9-11: "That Americans get to decide who is and who is not a terrorist means that this is not only a war without clear purpose, but also a war without end. From now on we can be in a perpetual state of war. America is always at her best when she is on permanent war footing. Moreover, when our country is at war, it has no space to worry about the extraordinary inequities that constitute our society, no time to worry about poverty or those parts of the world that are ravaged by hunger and genocide. Everything—civil liberties, due process, the protection of the law—must be subordinated to the one great moral enterprise of winning the unending war against terrorism." The question, "Will there ever be an end to the war on terror" is one worth pondering.

We hear many say, "What have we accomplished over the past thirteen years?" Furthermore, what does winning the war on terrorism look like? Do we have a moral obligation to fight forever? Another defining mark of the twenty-first century is the number of people who live in a constant state of fear and anxiety. The looming threat of terrorism fans the flame and keeps that fear alive. Hauerwas says: "As a pastor, my struggle is similar to everybody else's. I long for both peace and justice. But I do believe that there cannot be peace without justice. I struggle with how followers of the Prince of Peace can so quickly say, "bomb em." But a truth remains: we cannot and will not be able to have a civilized world if groups like ISIS are ignored. Religious extremism feeds itself on situations of hopelessness. And maybe that's where my real sadness lies: that there are so many people in the world who live such hopeless lives that they would succumb to such a perverted ideology and way of life.

91. Faith in a Post 9-11 World

What were you doing the day you heard the news about the twin towers? Where were you? Who told you? How did you feel? How long did it take for the reality to sink in?

September 11th, 2001 stands as a day that changed our nation, our world, and our individual mindsets forever. No longer did we feel safe in a homeland that is protected by oceans to the east, south, and west. No longer did many of us feel comfortable getting on a plane to travel from one destination to another. No longer did we feel at ease living our lives from day to day because paranoia had set in, and we became obsessed with thinking about what might happen next. That terrible day in our nation's history took the anxiety and fear that have always been a part of the human condition to a new level, and now, ten years later, many of us still live our lives worrying and fearful of what might happen next. Many of us live our lives obsessing, dreading, and anxious about the future and it keeps us from being able to enjoy the present.

It's hard to argue that we live in a post-911 world full of anxiety and fear. People worry about so many things, most of which will never happen. But true faith will enable us to stop our worrying, to trust in God, and to make the most of everyday that we are given. One of my Old Testament professors at Princeton had a favorite saying that he would always come back to in his lectures, and it was this: "Be not afraid." If there is one message that permeates the Bible from beginning to end, it is this, "Be not afraid." Have faith in the one who created you and don't let fear and anxiety keep you from living your life to the fullest. Be thankful for what you have, focus on the present, and your worries and fears will begin to subside.

92. Trump, Elitism and Middle America

We are now six months into the unscripted presidency of Donald J. Trump, and all we seem to hear about on the news is Russia. Of course, Paul Ryan and Mitch McConnell would remind us that there are other things happening within the halls of congress: health care reform, tax reform, a wall on the southern border, travel bans. But Russia's alleged ties to the Trump family continue to dominate the news cycle day in and day out. Here's a question: has anybody actually taken the time to seriously and objectively reflect upon what happened in this country in 2016? How did a billionaire businessman manage to become the spokesperson for the rust belt and blue collar Americans? How did he manage to dominate the Republican primaries and then take on and defeat the all-powerful Clinton machine? One word comes to mind: people are fed up with "elitism." Elitism is not being rich. Elitism is not going to Ivy League Schools. Elitism is not living in a particular neighborhood. Elitism happens on many socioeconomic levels and is prevalent within many university settings. It is the mindset that you are superior to, smarter than, and more sophisticated than other people, especially common people. Its only antidote is humility and perhaps, lost elections.

Political elitism among both Democrats and Republicans opened the door for Donald Trump, an outsider who had never held elected office before, to become the 45th President. Sure, there were other factors at play but this is what so many people seem to be missing and conveniently forgetting. In a May article for the *New Republic*, Michael Tomasky describes elitism as liberalism's biggest problem. There are clearly things that elitists simply don't get about those living in middle America. First, they go to church. God and Jesus play an important role in their lives, and they don't feel a need to apologize for their religion. Second, politics does not consume their lives. They don't sit around watching MSNBC every night and obsessing about the most recent conspiracy theory. They are working hard raising children, tending to their marriages, paying bills, and working to build the American Dream. Third, the lives of middle Americans are very different from the lives of elites. Many of them own guns to protect their families and believe strongly in the second Amendment. Fourth, middle Americans are deeply patriotic, and they don't badmouth the country in which they live. They are thankful for the chance to be here and enjoy the tremendous freedom and opportunity of this nation. Tomasky, who admits that he himself is a liberal elite, goes on to say that "this chasm between elite liberals and middle Americans is liberalism's biggest problem." Given the way things unfolded in 2016, I'd say he is right, but again, elitism is not limited to just one party.

Citizens can sense when a system is broken. People don't like to be talked down to and told how to think. People despise condescension and arrogance. Everybody gets a vote. You might ask, how could middle Americans choose Donald Trump as their guy? Isn't he an elite? Why did they come out in droves to support him? Were they just tired of business as usual? Yes. But more importantly, they had absolutely had it with the elitism of both political parties and wanted to send a disrupter to Washington. Now, we are watching to see how it unfolds.

93. Fixing Our Politics

Our culture has become more polarized, more hostile, more fearful, and more hateful. Why? There are many theories and reason. It could be the lack of community and authentic social interaction—read Robert Putnam's book *Bowling Alone*. It could be the bombardment of information in the digital age—people will say things on a screen they would never have the nerve of saying in person. It could be that politics has become a spectator sport, another form of entertainment television. It might simply be the fact that fear and anxiety is on the rise in the twenty-first century.

Whatever it is, something needs to be fixed. There are too many good people disappointed and disillusioned with this presidential race, regardless of party affiliation. I would argue that growing individualism leading to a sense of loneliness and isolation is also at the heart of the problem. Brooks says, "The individualist turn has accumulated a downside. By 2005, 47 percent of Americans reported that they knew none or just a few of their neighbors by name. There's been a sharp rise in the number of people who report that they have no close friends to confide in." Loneliness breeds fear. When politics becomes based on fear, hostility, hatred, and envy, the more important virtues disappear. Things like sacrifice, community, public service, bridge building, the common good, and patriotism begin to go by the wayside. Perhaps the greatest threat to our country does not come from the outside, ISIS or war weary refugees seeking a safe place to raise their children, but from the inside—the behavior of the American people and our leaders. If we expect civility and respect in our politics, then we must first show it ourselves. If we expect the gridlock to stop in Washington, then we must understand that compromise is part of the deal. If we expect moderates to have a chance at ever winning elections, then we must understand that the world is not black and white. There is a lot of grey. Who knows what the rest of this year will hold. It probably will not be pretty and many of us are already weary. But something must change in the way we go about this process. Something must change in the way we relate to each other. There is too much at stake. Civility, decency, and our children's futures come to mind.

94. Trump, the Pope, and American Politics

Pope Francis has now inserted himself into the circus that is this Presidential election. He had strong words regarding Donald Trump: "A person who thinks about only building walls, wherever they may be, and not building bridges, is not Christian." Wow. This puts Catholics who are supporting Trump in a real bind. We are now witnessing political polarization at its best. On one side, we have a socialist promising to pay for things his opponent says can't be delivered. On the other hand we have a billionaire who gives helicopter rides at the Iowa state fair and for whom Air Force One would be a down grade as a means of transportation. Many find themselves praying these will not be our only choices. A few years ago, I was preaching a sermon series on "Christianity and Capitalism," acknowledging the fact that there is healthy tension that exists between the two if we take the words of Jesus seriously. The two can and certainly do coexist in American culture, but I consider Christianity to be the conscience of capitalism in many ways. In between the two services on that particular Sunday, somebody blindsided me with a question: "Do you think it's possible the tension exists because Jesus was a socialist?" To be honest, that question caught me off guard because socialism did not exist until the nineteenth century. I don't think Jesus was a socialist, but I would acknowledge that some of his teachings and parables have socialist overtones. It would be fascinating to hear Jesus' thoughts on modern day capitalism and the free market. What would he think of Trump, Sanders, Hillary, or Cruz?

Here is a perplexing question: "Was Jesus political?" The obvious answer for many scholars has always been a resounding "yes," which then leads to the following questions: "What type of politics did he advocate for, and what type of politics would he advocate today." Would he be a Democrat? Would he be a Republican? Would he just be independent? Christian leaders on both the political left and the right claim to be the "true Christians." Jim Wallis is just as passionate about his views regarding poverty and war as Jerry Falwell once was regarding homosexuality and abortion. Since both can't be right on issues where they adamantly disagree, who should we believe? Who are the real Christians? For many pastors, the debate and polarization are exhausting. We live in interesting times, and this is an interesting year.

In their book *American Grace*, Robert Putnam and David Campbell say this regarding politics and religion: "American history teaches us that religion is neither exclusively left nor right, progressive nor conservative. Instead, religion of different sorts has been associated with political causes of different sorts. On some issues, notably those related to race, religion has been invoked to justify both sides of the debate. In the nineteenth century, religion animated advocates of both abolition and slavery. No one made the point better than Abraham Lincoln, who, in his second inaugural address, referred to the two sides of the Civil War by noting that "both read the same Bible and pray to the same God, and each invokes his aid against the other." Wherever we may find ourselves on the ideological spectrum, 2016 is a year we will all find ourselves wrestling with this relationship and the many ways it manifests itself. Life in America is anything but boring.

95. Living in a 5-4 World

When the Supreme Court made its 5-4 ruling on same sex marriage, I immediately thought less about my own perspective and more about what it will mean for the future of Christianity and the church. Many already claim that we live in a post-Christian world where the church has lost its influence in society. Some point to this ruling as clear evidence that the church has not done its job. Others say the ruling will now give the church a chance to reach people it has alienated and marginalized from the pews for years. Both use scripture to defend their position. My fear all along has been an increased polarization within Christianity. There are churches who are adamantly against same sex marriage, and they are digging in. There are churches who are adamantly for it, and they will raise the flag even higher. What about those of us who pastor churches where not everybody agrees?

We say in the Christian Church that we "agree to disagree." "In essentials, unity; in non-essentials, liberty; but in all things, love." Christianity would do well to make this issue a non-essential and let good people simply disagree. United Methodist pastor Travis Garner wrote these pastoral words the Sunday following the ruling regarding the complexity of the situation: "When we proclaim from our soapboxes that you're either in favor of this decision or you're a hateful bigot, we're being shortsighted. When we say you're either against this decision or you're championing immorality, we're failing to understand the complex reality in which we find ourselves." Make no mistake, these are complicated times. Passions run high. Fear is pervasive. Anger is real. On Friday, June 26th, many celebrated the court's decision as justice long overdue. Others felt as though five activist judges had spoken for the people and had no right to redefine marriage. Garner also wrote this: "As a pastor, I'm a pastor to both the 5 and to the 4. I'm a pastor to people who sharply disagree with one another. And the bottom line is this: all are welcomed in my church and loved unconditionally by God. And all are asked and enabled to become more than what they are when they walked in the door—a person who is continually growing and transforming into the likeness of Christ. I am grateful that this morning, at my church, there will be space for everyone; all are invited."

All are entitled to their own beliefs regarding marriage and what it is, and the church would be well-served to be a place where civil and respectful dialogue can occur. Demonizing those with whom we disagree is never a good idea. The Apostle Paul identifies the fruit of the spirit in Galatians 5: love, joy, peace, patience, kindness, generosity, faithfulness, gentleness, and self-control. What you will not find on this list is anger, hatred, resentment, fear, hostility, pride, or bitterness. Wherever Christians might stand on this issue, let us not lose sight of Christ and his commandment to love.

(Published July 4, 2015)

96. Faith in a World of Terrorism

Our hearts break for the families who have lost loved ones in Paris. Once again, we have been painfully reminded that we live in a dangerous world where religious extremists are willing to kill and massacre in the name of God. These were innocent people living their lives, going to dinner, attending a soccer match, listening to live music at a concert hall. These were husbands and wives, mothers and fathers, sons and daughters. It is sickening and infuriating. They had no idea that Friday, November 13th, would be their final day. How are we to respond? It is clear that these religious extremists have no interest in peace. They have no interest in dialogue. They have no interest in respecting human life or the ways of the civilized world. This is the twenty-first century face of evil, and you cannot rationalize with evil. Dietrich Bonhoeffer was one of the great church leaders in the early 20th century. He believed in community. He believed in peace. He believed in the ways and teachings of Christ. However, when confronted with the reality that was Adolf Hitler and the Third Reich, he went in on an assassination plot. He felt that there is only one way to deal with that type of evil. In 2018, ISIS is an evil that must be dealt with. Their goal is not only a global caliphate, but also for all of us to live paralyzed by fear. We cannot let them succeed. One of Christ's pervading messages was "be not afraid." That message is more relevant today than ever before. We cannot live our lives in a state of fear because that's exactly what they want, and that's exactly what we cannot give them.

I was moved by the words of a young husband and father who lost his wife in the Paris attacks. Here was Antoine Leiris's message to ISIS: "Friday night you took away the life of an exceptional human being, the love of my life, the mother of my son, but you will not have my hatred. I do not know who you are, and I do not wish to. You are dead souls. If this God for whom you kill so blindly has made us in His image, every bullet in the body of my wife will have been a wound in His heart. So I will not give you the privilege of hating you. You certainly sought it, but replying to hatred with anger would be giving in to the same ignorance which made you into what you are. You want me to be frightened, that I should look into the eyes of my fellow citizens with distrust, that I sacrifice my freedom for security. You lost. I will carry on as before. I saw her this morning. Finally, after nights and days of waiting. She was as beautiful as when she left on Friday evening, as beautiful as when I fell madly in love with her more than 12 years ago. I am of course devastated by heartbreak, I'll cede you that little victory, but it will be short-lived. I know that she will be with us every day and that we will meet again in a paradise of free souls to which you will never have access." ISIS wants all of us to live in fear. Let's do the opposite.

97. Money, Time, and the American Way

Presbyterian Pastor Eugene Peterson makes a bold yet honest statement in his pastoral memoir: "I love being an American. I love this place in which I have been placed—its language, its history, its energy. But I don't love 'the American Way,' its culture and values. I don't love the rampant consumerism that treats God as a product to be marketed. I don't love the dehumanizing ways that turn men, women, and children into impersonal roles and causes and statistics. I don't love the competitive spirit that treats others as rivals and even as enemies." When our nation was established, Thomas Jefferson and the Founders famously wrote that all are entitled to "life, liberty, and the pursuit of happiness." We all approach that "pursuit" differently. Here's a fact: If I didn't know you and wanted to learn what's most important in your life, I could ask for your calendar and your bank statement. We communicate our priorities and values in life by the way we spend our time and money. We make decisions regarding those two things each and every day.

Jesus had more to say about wealth, money, and possessions than almost any other subject during his life and ministry. He knew it was a stumbling block then, and it still is today. Preachers who find themselves in affluent pulpits preaching to wealthy and powerful church members will always feel the tension of "walking the tightrope" when it comes to preaching and teaching about money. Many of the scripture passages are difficult to hear and may even come across as threatening to those living comfortably. Yet, if challenged and encouraged, the wealthy have the means and capability to change and even save lives. Pastors who find themselves in poorer churches must find a way to give hope and comfort to those who are struggling to make ends meet. Many often forget how inadequate people feel when they don't have enough money to pay their bills, put food on the table, or take care of their families.

Pastors have a difficult job: to balance the realities of capitalism and the ongoing competitive pursuit of the American Dream (defined differently by everyone) while also warning against greed, materialism, narcissism, and selfishness, all of which can lead to spiritual suicide. Simply avoiding the subject of money is not an option if we seek to be faithful to the gospel. I've heard it many times before: "When you talk about money, it makes me uncomfortable." To which I can say, "Well, take it up with Jesus." Money and possessions should be talked about and Jesus knew that. In some churches, money talk is taboo, but why? We live in a culture that is obsessed with money, driven by money, and focused on money. On the one hand, money is a universal reality and necessity. But money also means power and influence, accomplishment and prestige. Money is often the way we judge the value of a person and whether they have been successful in life. Money drives political passions, perspectives, and elections. The Great Recession brought the subject of money and materialism to the forefront, and it became an excellent teaching moment for preachers to focus on priorities and what really matters in life. The stock market plunged, banks collapsed, corruption scandals were unveiled, retirement accounts were cut in half, and millions of jobs were lost. Everybody was affected in one way or another. Fear was widespread, and many are still afraid. Money makes a great servant in life, but it makes a terrible master. If we allow our money to serve us and the things that we want to support, that is good. But if we are enslaved to our money and to the accumulation of wealth and possessions, if we are always comparing ourselves to others, restlessness and discontentment are likely. The only people who know that money is not the secret to happiness are those who have plenty of it and are still miserable. Some of the happiest and most joy-filled people in our world are those who have little or nothing and may not know it. Possessions can become possessive very quickly.

However, in reality, there is something much more important than money: time. Money is not a substitute for time, especially time spent with those we love. Time is far more valuable. We can't get it back. We can't push rewind. Time is a precious gift, yet many of us take it for granted and fail to live in the moment. We're busy texting, tweeting, and surfing the web on our phones with our children growing up before our very eyes. Life seems to happen while we are distracted and making other plans. The late Steve Jobs once said: "Your time is limited, so don't waste it living someone else's life. Don't be trapped by dogma — which is living with the results of other people's thinking. Don't let the noise of others' opinions drown out your own inner voice. And most important, have the courage to follow your heart and intuition. They somehow already know what you truly want to become. Everything else is secondary." Jobs lived the American dream but seemed to enjoy it along the way. Jesus said, "What will you profit you to gain the whole world but forfeit your life? And what can you give in return for your life" (Matt 16:26).

VI

EVENTS IN THE NEWS

98. Aurora Shootings Serve as Reality Check

Last Friday, July 20th, I awoke early in the morning to watch the second round of the British open. Specifically, I wanted to watch Nashville player Brandt Snedeker who was in the lead and playing some incredible golf. As I turned the TV to ESPN, I heard the announcer say that America would be waking up to some very tragic news. I quickly turned the channel to CNN to see what had happened and found out what took place just a few hours earlier in theatre number nine in Aurora, CO. At the midnight showing of the new Batman movie, twenty-four-year-old James Holmes had entered the theatre dressed as the Joker. He was wearing a gas mask, bullet proof vest, and other protective gear. He had three different guns. After setting off canisters of tear gas, he opened fire on a theatre full of innocent people. He killed twelve people and injured over fifty others. At the time, it was the worst mass shooting in American history.

Like so many others, I have been thinking about this constantly, the families who lost loved ones including a six-year-old little girl. The magnitude and devastation of this event is mind boggling. The pain and sense of loss is overwhelming. Why do these things happen? What happened in Aurora, CO can and should serve as a reality check for all of us.

First, it should teach us that life can end at any minute. James says, "The length of your life is as uncertain as the morning mist. Now you see it, soon it is gone." It may be a deranged gunman. It may be a car accident. It may be cancer or a heart attack that does it. Life is fragile, and there is no guarantee about tomorrow. Those who entered the theatre that night had absolutely no idea what was about to happen.

The victims had no idea they would not leave the theatre alive. The families had no idea they would not see their loved ones again. One lunatic with red hair has caused so much loss, pain, and grief, and nobody saw it coming. Life is to be lived to the fullest each and every day because we never know when our time on this earth will be up.

Secondly, the outpouring of love and support from all over the country and from around the world reminds us that good will always trump evil. The families who have lost loved ones are not struggling alone. We all feel their pain. It could have been anybody's son, daughter, husband, wife, brother, or sister in that theatre. The good of humanity always comes out in the wake of tragedy.

Third, it is time we have a serious conversation about gun laws in this country. I've heard all the arguments of both sides. I've read the second amendment in the Constitution about the right to bear arms. I have lots of friends who like to hunt. I know the NRA is a force to be reckoned with. I get it. But we all know there is a difference between a hand gun or rifle and an AK 47. Nobody needs that for hunting or for self-defense. And just watch, this subject will not be talked about by the President or the Republican nominee, not because they don't care about it, but because we're three months away from an election. Something must change here. It's simply too easy for people to buy guns and ammunition.

Lastly, as we continue the conversation about health care in our country, we have to be intentional about dealing with mental illness because it is real. A very big part of being healthy at any age is being mentally healthy and just deciding to not cover that area of care should not be an option. We have made many advances in the field of mental health but there are still some who like to pretend it isn't real. It is real.

Jesus said, "Blessed are those who mourn, for they will be comforted." We ask God's blessing on all those whose lives were lost and those who were injured. We won't forget you. We love you. God bless you.

(Published July 28, 2012)

99. Remembering Clementa Pinckney

Rev. Clementa C. Pinckney was born July 30, 1973 in Ridgeland, SC. He was educated in the public schools of Jasper Country and graduated magna cum laude from Allen University with a degree in Business Administration where he served as class president and president of the student body. He was a Woodrow Wilson summer research fellow at Princeton, earned a Master's degree from the University of South Carolina in public administration, and a Master of Divinity from Lutheran Theological Southern Seminary. A natural born leader, he was called to preach at thirteen, became a pastor at eighteen, was elected to the South Carolina House of Representatives at twenty-three, and then to the State Senate at twenty-seven. He did this while also serving as pastor of Emanuel AME Church in Charleston. He was a loving husband and father of two daughters. This was a truly remarkable man, committed to God, family, and to serving the common good. On Wednesday night, June 17th, while leading a Bible study at his church in Charleston, he and eight others became the victims of a senseless hate crime because of the color of their skin and where they happened to be. His killer, Dylann Roof, a twenty-one-year-old white supremacist with hate in his heart, wanted to start a race war by killing black people. He achieved the opposite. Emanuel AME Church, Charleston, and our nation now stand in solidarity in the aftermath of this horrific tragedy.

It's hard to believe that there are still people like Roof in this country, a clear indication that all racism is not generational. Where does this hate originate? Why is it there? What can we do about it? The fact that he could sit in a Bible study for an hour, interacting with those he was about to execute, is unfathomable and evil. Our thoughts and prayers remain with Pinckney's wife and daughters, the families of all the victims, and the members of Emanuel AME Church. Good is coming out of this tragedy. Hope is taking the place of despair. Love is winning. It is now up to all of us to take the torch from Rev. Pinckney and advance the causes he was so passionate about. Let us work diligently to build to bridges and tear down walls of fear that divide and polarize. Let us work together for the common good, looking out for the least of these in our society. Let us remember the words of Dr. King who said, "Hate cannot drive out hate. Only love can do that." Let us remember that just sticking to "our community" or "our side of town" is not enough. We must come together and build relationships with those different from us. Let us also remember the timeless words of Christ: "This is my commandment, that you love one another as I have loved you. No one has greater love than this, to lay down one's life for one's friends." That is exactly what Rev. Pinckney did on that dreadful night in Charleston: He laid down his life for his friends. His death will not be in vain!

100. Vegas, Guns, God, and Peace

What happened in Las Vegas was an absolute tragedy, but I don't want to hear Pat Robertson or anybody else saying it was the will of God or punishment for a sinful city. That is the kind of theological garbage that drives people away from faith. This was simply the result of God granting human beings the ability to make our own decisions, and this guy chose to plan and commit a horrendous act of evil. These were sons and daughters, husbands and wives, children and grandchildren, good people living their lives. Now, many of those lives are over with their families grieving and picking up the pieces. Words are simply inadequate in trying to describe what happened. Our culture has become desensitized to violence. It no longer takes us by surprise. To say we have a gun problem in this country is like saying Nashville has a traffic problem. We all know it's true, but will we do anything about it?

The Second Amendment of the Constitution is not a black and white issue. There are nuanced positions that require reason and compromise. Sensible laws could be passed and provisions made that might prevent these kinds of attacks in the future. And if they don't, at least we can say we tried. Buck up congress! How many innocent people have to die? No other civilized country has this kind of carnage on the streets. An overwhelming majority of American gun owners support sensible restrictions, yet we still can't seem to get them in place. A larger concern continues to be the growing lack of peace and civility in our culture, starting at the top. There is too much hate, too much anger, too much loneliness, too much fear, too much resentment, and too much rage. These are all clear signs of a nation in a spiritual crisis.

Spiritual emptiness and isolation is a universal disease. What can we do to change this? It starts with listening to one another, loving one another, building community, serving one another, and respecting our differences. Peace begins in the heart and grows from there. You can't spread peace until you first find it yourself. It also starts with our leaders growing up and acting like leaders. After the tragedy at Sandy Hook, Archbishop Charles Chaput offered these words: "God is good, but we human beings are free, and being free we help fashion the nature of our world with the choices we make…We're free, and therefore responsible for the beauty and the suffering we help make. Why does God allow wickedness? He allows it because we—or others like us—choose it. The only effective antidote to the wickedness around us is to live differently from this moment forward." Human beings are not puppets. We have free will. We don't understand why Las Vegas happened. On the surface, it doesn't make any sense. But all of us can do our part to help bring more peace, love, and hope into this world. I think we can all agree that our world needs much more of that!

101. Lessons from Ferguson, Missouri

Since the grand jury's announcement Monday night not to indict Officer Darren Wilson in the shooting of eighteen-year-old Michael Brown, we have all been watching the news: the violence, anger, outrage, looting, fires, protesting, spin, and the chaos. This situation is indicative of an ongoing problem in our culture: dualistic thinking. It's the belief that you are either racist and think that Darren Wilson did nothing wrong or you are not racist and feel that Michael Brown's life was taken unjustly. Pardon the pun, but the world is not just black and white. There has always been a lot of grey, and the truth is usually found somewhere in the middle.

I have been amazed at the number of people who decided from the outset that they knew exactly what happened on that fateful summer day in Ferguson. I have been just as amazed at the number of people who still deny that racism continues to be a problem in our culture. I was born and raised in Memphis, TN, a town that has racial tension in its history and DNA. King's assassination on April 4, 1968 left a permanent mark on Memphis that has never been overcome despite the valiant efforts of many. King had a famous dream that one day his children would live in a nation where people would be judged not by the color of their skin but by the content of their character. That's a world we should all long for and embrace, but how are we doing with that? Six years into the first African American presidency, how are race relations in our nation? Have we made significant progress? I have always believed that racism is rooted in fear, ignorance, and an unwillingness to get to know those who are different. Socio-economic status also plays a major role. Racism and classism breaks the heart of God. We read in I Samuel, "Mortals look on the outward appearance, but the Lord looks on the heart."

Are there lessons from what has transpired in Ferguson? I think so. We have a criminal justice system that is far from perfect but that still must be allowed to run its course. What other options do we have? Trial by popular opinion? Racial representation is certainly important within law enforcement, but is not always as easy as some might suggest. Ferguson must address this. Laws and law enforcement must be respected and obeyed for the sake of order, safety, and civility. Rioting, violence, and looting is no way to respond to a grand jury's decision. Many were simply waiting for the opportunity to go and wreak havoc, and they did. There are peaceful and more productive ways to protest. Lastly, it is clear that we still have a long way to go in terms of race relations in this country. Muhammad Ali said it well, "Hating people because of their color is wrong. And it doesn't matter which color does the hating. It's just plain wrong." Former Secretary General of the UN Kofi Annan articulates a worthwhile goal: "Ignorance and prejudice are the handmaidens of propaganda. Our mission, therefore, is to confront ignorance with knowledge, bigotry with tolerance, and isolation with the outstretched hand of generosity. Racism can, will, and must be defeated." Let us all pray for Ferguson regardless of how we may feel.

102. Pulse Night Club—Good Religion, Bad Religion

What took place in Orlando last Sunday morning at the Pulse night club was an absolute tragedy. Not only was it a horrendous act of terror, the worst mass shooting in our nation's history. It was also an act of hate, directed at the gay community. Fifty people were killed including the shooter, and many more remain injured in the hospital. Robert Lynch, a Catholic Bishop from St. Petersburg wrote these words that appeared in the Washington Post: "Even before I knew who perpetrated the mass murders at Pulse, I knew that somewhere in the story, there would be a search for religion as motivation. While deranged people do senseless things, all of us observe and judge and act from some kind of religious background. Singling out people for victimization because of their religion, their sexual orientation, their nationality must be offensive to God's ears. It has to stop."

In his new book called *Flourishing: Why We Need Religion in a Globalized World*, Yale theologian Miroslav Volf says that religion is an inevitable part of the globalization process, but it's very complicated in the twenty-first century. And the answer to bad religion is not no religion. The answer to bad religion is good religion. He says, "World religions are our most potent sources of moral motivation and deliberation. They are also carriers of visions of the good life, which billions have found compelling throughout history and still find compelling today. Central to these visions is the paramount importance of transcendence, of the invisible realm, of God—but not as a mysterious power outside the world. Relation to that transcendent realm fundamentally shapes how we understand and relate to our world and ourselves."

In the wake of these types of tragedies, there are always those who say, "Religion is the problem." Religion is not the problem. Bad religion, perverted religion, distorted religion, radical religion grounded in hate and intolerance, is the problem. The only answer to this is healthy religion, religion that fosters tolerance and respect, peace and love, compassion and empathy. This is what our world needs, and we are called to spread it. Those who walked into that night club last Saturday night had no idea that their lives were about to come to a violent end. They were targeted for who they were. Their lives were cut short. The hate that was displayed has now backfired and has been turned inside out. When ask by a lawyer about the greatest commandment of all, Jesus had two responses: "Love God with all your heart, soul, mind, and strength. Love your neighbor as yourself." Everything else is secondary.

(Published June 18, 2016)

103. Parkland Shooting Points to Larger Spiritual Problems

On Wednesday, a grieving father stood before President Trump at the White House and with anger and rage in his voice asked, "How many schools and how many children have to be shot in this country before we do something? I'm here today because my daughter has no voice. She was murdered last week, taken from us, shot nine times." That same night, Senator Marco Rubio walked into a heated town hall gathering in Sunrise, FL where he faced the same question from parents, family, and surviving students of the mass shooting at Marjory Stoneman Douglas High School. Rubio was clearly rattled. How could he not be? Talking points were not going to cut it with this group. One of the major problems in this country is binary thinking, a belief that everything is black and white. You are either for guns or you're not. You either support the NRA or you don't. You either believe in the Second Amendment or you don't. You're either a conservative or a liberal. If only life were that simple. There are nuanced positions in life that require reason, courage, compromise, and emotional intelligence. How many innocent children have to die in their classrooms before we try a different approach? And if we try something else and it still happens, at least we will have tried. No other civilized country in the world has this kind of carnage. I thought something would surely change after Sandy Hook when six-year-olds were shot and killed. It didn't. I thought something would surely change after Las Vegas. It didn't.

We like to turn these things into partisan fights which reveals our tribalism and immaturity. Now, let's be clear. Gun control is not the only issue at hand. Mental illness, background checks, bad parenting, missed intelligence, school security, the legal age to purchase firearms, and congressional cowardice should all be talked about. And yes, this is all related to larger issues in the culture, spiritual issues, moral issues. There continues to be too much hate, anger, resentment, incivility, loneliness, fear, and rage. These are indicators of a society in spiritual crisis.

Billy Graham said over and over again, "Our nation needs a spiritual reawakening." He was convinced of it. He spent his entire life traveling the nation and the globe to lead that charge. Graham knew all too well that emptiness and isolation is real for far too many. Our purpose is found in loving God and loving each other. A spiritual reawakening takes courage, hope, and a desire to unite and not divide. Families must remain strong. Parents must recognize that their role is essential. Education must be funded. Digital devices cannot become substitutes for face to face community. Relationships remain at the core. We must listen to one another, love one another, reach out to those who hurt, build friendships with those who are strangers, serve those in need, and learn to respect our differences. Morality matters. Everything is not relative. We must recognize that we are all made in God's image with intrinsic value and worth. But for the sake of these seventeen kids and coaches killed on Valentine's Day. For the sake of the fifty-eight victims killed on the Las Vegas strip. For the sake of the fifty killed at Pulse night club in Orlando. For the sake of the twenty students and six teachers killed at Sandy Hook Elementary. For the sake of San Bernadino, Columbine, Aurora, Fort Hood, and all the others that we can list, let's do something to create a healthier culture and world where this does not happen.

104. Penn State Scandal Teaches Many Lessons

Like the rest of the country, I have been absolutely floored to hear the details of the Penn State saga continue to unfold. In an age where sex scandals have become a part of the regular news cycle, this one takes it to new heights. Although he will be given due process and his day in court, the accusations regarding the actions of former assistant coach Jerry Sandusky are despicable and unfathomable. The report of the grand jury will make you angry and sick at the same time. We should all pray for the victims and their families who have been through so much. There is the trauma from the incidents that happened years ago and then the trauma of reliving it through the media frenzy in recent weeks.

Since the news first started to break, I have been reflecting on the moral lessons that this sad situation teaches, and there are quite a few. If there is one thing that can come from travesties like this, it is education and awareness. First of all, let this be a lesson to all sexual predators who prey on innocent, young children that you will be caught. It may be years later, but the truth will come out, and justice will be done. Secondly, as exciting and lucrative as college football might be (and I'm a big fan), it must hold its proper place in a University setting. A famous football program or coach is never a reason to cover up a scandal or look the other way. Joe Paterno is now learning a very difficult lesson after an amazing career: there is a difference between a moral obligation and a legal obligation. Too many schools are dominated and run by their football programs, and this can be a problem on many levels. Thirdly, by state law, anybody who is aware of sexual misconduct regarding a minor has a legal and moral obligation to report it to authorities. The way to prevent this type of thing from happening in the future is for communities to work together to look out for our most vulnerable—children. And lastly, institutions (churches, schools, etc.) must do everything in their power to make sure that their children are safe and protected. The statistics are amazing regarding sexual abuse in our culture, and incidents like this can ruin a child psychologically and emotionally. They will carry the hurt and baggage the rest of their lives. Communities and institutions must work together to protect our children.

When a story of this magnitude breaks, there is shock, disbelief, anger, and deep sadness. Over time we will continue to watch it unfold and continue to share these same emotions. The reputation of Penn State has been tarnished. The legacy of Joe Paterno, a man that has been worshipped by many, is certainly now in question. We must use this as an opportunity to warn potential predators, educate our society, keep college athletics in their proper place, and commit ourselves to protecting innocent children.

105. Syrian Dilemma Divides People of Faith

The situation in Syria is serious and very complicated at the same time. Civil War has been raging in that country for years, and now our intelligence tells us that the Assad regime has used chemical weapons against its own people, breaking international law, and murdering thousands of innocent people, including children in the Damascus area. Millions are living as refugees in various parts of the country. Once again, the US has a difficult decision to make, and it's basically between the lesser of two evils. Do we turn the other way, or do we get involved? And if we get involved, to what degree? As in so many other situations, people of faith are divided over what to do. Given the events of the past decade, I do think it is wise for us to take the time to really think this one through. We are a war-weary country. Many would also argue that we are broke, so whatever we do is on borrowed money. There is no easy answer here, and we should beware of those who say that there is.

Stanley Hauerwas is an ethicist at Duke University, and he is an outspoken pacifist. I do not agree with everything he has to say, but I have a lot of respect for his relentless advocacy for peace in light of his Christian faith. A few years ago, he wrote a book titled *War and the American Difference* (2011). In that book, he says, "For Americans, war is necessary to sustain our belief that we are worthy to be recipients of the sacrifices made on our behalf in past wars. Americans are a people born of and in war, particularly the Civil War, and only war can sustain our belief that we are a people set apart" (Hauerwas 27). In regard to the Syrian situation, he recently said this: "What possible grounds does the United

States have for intervention? The language of the world's policeman comes up again. You want to know, 'Who appointed
you the world's policeman?' You could say the U.S. can justify the intervention because stability is part of our foreign
policy in order to maintain ourselves as the premier country
in the world. So it's smart to intervene. But there's no moral
justification." Many disagree and believe there is moral justification. That's why this is hard.

What do we do about leaders like Assad? Is it our responsibility to sort it out, and if so, where does it stop? Throughout history, "Just War Theory" has been used when trying
to justify the use of force. Dating back to the early church
fathers like Augustine and Aquinas, Just War Theory seeks
to answer the following questions before force is used. Is the
war being waged as a last resort? Is it being waged by a legitimate authority? Is it addressing a wrong suffered? Is there a
reasonable chance of success? Can peace be reestablished? Is
the violence in the war proportional to the injuries suffered?
Can we discriminate between combatants and non-combat-
ants? In terms of Syria, many believe that we cannot answer
"yes" to each of these questions. Again, what should we do?

Andrew Bacevich, a professor of international studies at
Boston University recently said this: "What do we expect to
achieve? Even if there is a moral case for intervention, how
does the use of force remedy the situation? It appears to me
that this is going to be a very limited attack with a very limited target set. There's no intention of overthrowing the regime
and no intention of limiting the chemical weapons capability
of the Syrian Army. So beyond allowing ourselves to feel vir-
tuous because we have done something in response to a rep-
rehensible act, what has been gained? If indeed the episode

in Syria rises to the level where it is different from Egypt, and we really are morally obligated to do something, then it ought to be something more than just a gesture. And, of course, as a practical matter, nobody's got the appetite to do anything more than make gestures." In recent years, I have grown increasingly skeptical of those who are quick to beat war drums. War is absolute hell. Anybody who has fought in a war will tell you that. Personally, I don't question the moral motives of those who want to deal with a guy like Assad. They see evil and want justice. What he did and continues to do is unfathomable. What I struggle with is the reality of how things will play out. We need to learn lessons from the past ten years and ask ourselves what we hope to accomplish here.

106. Lessons from 2017

We are about to turn the page on 2017 and what a year it has been! The New Year is an ideal time to reflect and to look ahead. What will we remember from this year? Trump's Inauguration? The Women's March on Washington? Travel bans debated in the courts? Political uprisings in Europe? The aggression of North Korea? The suicide bombing at a concert in Manchester? The removal of Confederate monuments? The march in Charlottesville? The firing of James Comey? The ongoing FBI investigation? The surging stock market? The Las Vegas massacre? The Harvey Weinstein scandal and the "Me Too" movement? Matt Lauer's fall from glory? A church shooting in a small Texas town? Political incivility? Roy Moore's rise and defeat? Tax legislation? This has been quite a year. Perhaps the most important lessons have to do with morality and ethics and should be posed in the form of questions. Is it right to ban travel to the United States from predominately Muslim countries for the sake of national security? Does the war on terror ever actually end? Why has sexual assault been acceptable for so many years? Is our justice department truly "nonpartisan"? Why is there such racial tension fifty years after the civil rights movement? Will we ever address the assault weapon problem? Can civility be restored to the public square? What is the proper role of government? Does character matter in politics?

These are tough questions, but the way we talk about them and the conclusions we reach matter. It's been said before that "those who forget history are bound to repeat it." Human beings seem to have a short memory. The most important lessons we can learn are often the most obvious: the way we treat one another and the way we function together as a society matters. We should work to avoid certain things in our personal lives and interactions: selfishness, arrogance, condescension, hatred, anger, envy, bitterness, indifference, and resentment. We should work for the well-being of all. The message of Christmas must remain into the New Year: hope, peace, joy, and love. These virtues are timeless and should guide how we live our lives. Character matters. Words and tone matter. Confronting our fears and managing our anger matters. Most importantly, we must not be afraid to change, grow, live and to act differently. To become superior to our former selves. We must continue to wrestle with the difficult questions that remain. Life is what we make of it, and every day we get to decide how we want to live. Values must be taught, modeled, and then sustained. The right attitude is essential.

Bibliography

Borg, Marcus J. *Convictions: How I Learned What Matters Most*. New York: Harper Collins, 2015.

Brooks, David. *The Road To Character*. New York: Random House, 2015.

Brown, Peter. *St Augustine of Hippo: A Biography*. Berkeley: University of California Press, 1969.

Christiansen, Clayton R. *How Will You Measure Your Life?* New York: Harper Business, 2012.

Colglazier, R. Scott. *Finding a Faith that Makes Sense*. St. Louis: Chalice Press, 1996.

Corley, Benjamin. *Unafraid: Moving Beyond a Fear Based Faith*. New York: Harper One, 2017.

Cron, Ian and Susan Stabile. *The Road Back to You*. Downers Grove, IL: InterVarsity Press, 2016.

Cox, Harvey. *The Future of Faith*. New York: Harper Collins, 20009.

Frankl, Victor E. *Man's Search for Meaning*. Boston, Beacon Press, 1992 (original manuscript 1946).

Friedman, Edwin. *A Failure of Nerve*. Church Publishing Inc., 2007.

Haidt, Jonathan. *The Happiness Hypothesis*. New York: Basic Books, 2006.

Haidt, Jonathan. *The Righteous Mind*. New York: Pantheon Books, 2012.

Hanh, *The Art of Living*. New York: Harper Collins, 2017.

Hari, Johann. *Lost Connections*. New York: Bloomsbury USA, 2018.

Hauerwas, Stanley and Will Willimon. *The Truth About God: The Ten Commandments in Christian Life*. Nashville: Abington Press, 1999.

Hauerwas, Stanley. "Can Greed Be a Good?" *Religion and Ethics*, June 9, 2010. Accessed December 8, 2014. http://www.abc.net.au/religion/articles/2010/06/09/2922773.htm.

Hauerwas, Stanley. *The Peaceable Kingdom*. University of Notre Dame Press, 1983.

Jarvis, F. Washington. *With Love and Prayers: A Headmaster Speaks to the Next Generation*. Boston: David. R. Godine, 2000.

Keller, Timothy. *Counterfeit Gods*. New York: Dutton, 2009.

Kushner, Harold. *Overcoming Life's Disappointments*. New York: Alfred A. Knopf, 2006.

Lama, Dalai and Desmond Tutu. *The Book of Joy: Lasting Happiness in a Changing World*. New York: Avery, 2016.

Meacham, Jon. *American Gospel: God, The Founding Fathers and the Making of a Nation*. New York: Random House, 2006.

Peck, M. Scott. *The Road Less Traveled*. New York: Simon & Schuster, 1978.

Peterson, Eugene. *The Pastor*. New York: Harper One, 2011.

Petersen, Jordan. *12 Rules for Life: An Antidote to Chaos*. Toronto: Random House Canada, 2018.

Putnam, Robert D. *Bowling Alone: The Collapse and Revival of American Community*. New York: Simon & Schuster, 2000.

Rohr, Richard. *Jesus' Plan for a New World: The Sermon on the Mount*. Cincinnati, Franciscan Media, 1996.

Rohr, Richard. *Everything Belongs*. New York: Crossroads Publishing, 2003.

Sacks, Jonathan. *Not In God's Name: Confronting Religious Violence*. New York: Schocken Books, 2015.

Sasse, Ben. *Them: Why We Hate Each Other and How To Heal*. New York: St. Martin's Press, 2018.

Scazzero, Peter. *Emotionally Healthy Spirituality*. Grand Rapids: Zondervan, 2006.

Schuller, Robert. *The Be Happy Attitudes*. Waco: Word Books, 1985.

Schulz, Kathryn. *On Being Wrong: Adventures in the Margin of Error*. New York: Harper Collins, 2010.

Shelly, Rubel. *I Knew Jesus Before He Was a Christian*. Abilene: Leafwood Publishers, 2011.

Simmons, Richard E. *The True Measure of a Man*. Mobile: Evergreen Press, 2011.

Simmons, Richard E. *Wisdom: Life's Great Treasure*. Birmingham: Union Hill Publishing, 2016.

Sittser, Jerry. *A Grace Disguised: How the Soul Grows Through Loss* (Expanded Edition) Grand Rapids: Zondervan Press, 2004.

Slaughter, Mike, Charles Gutenson, and Robert Jones. *Hijacked: Responding to the Partisan Church Divide*. Nashville: Abington Press, 2012.

Smith, Douglas A. *Happiness: The Art of Living with Peace, Confidence, and Joy*. Columbus: White Pine Mountain, 2014.

The Holy Bible (New Revised Standard Version). Grand Rapids: Zondervan Publishing House, 1989.

Taylor, Charles. *A Secular Age*. Cambridge: Harvard Press, 2007.

Vance, J.D. *Hillbilly Elegy*. New York: Harper Collins, 2016.

Volf, Miroslav. *Flourishing Why We Need Religion in a Globalized World*. New Haven: Yale University Press, 2015.

Willimon, William H. *Why Jesus?* Nashville: Abington Press, 2010.

Wright, Nicholas Thomas. *Simply Jesus*. New York: Harper One, 2011.